About *The Wholehearted Church Planter*

"Linda and Allan's new book cuts right to the heart of church planting. Church planting is truly for everyone. Not only that, it is the task for the normal follower of Jesus and not simply for the highly educated, the entrepreneurial, the skilled, the charismatic leader, or the alpha male. *The Wholehearted Church Planter* pulls back the layers of what we assume church planting is about and rescues the conversation from merely techniques and strategies. It is about a life of wholehearted devotion to God where church planting becomes more of a lifestyle rather than a job or applying the right tactics. This book liberates church planting from professionalism and places it back into the hands of everyday disciples."

■ Sean Benesh, director of the Epoch Center and author of *View From the Urban Loft*

"Linda and Allan remind us that church planting is not rocket science; it comes down to knowing and loving God, people, and the place to which God has sent you. This book is your invitation to join God in making disciples, for as you do that, you might discover that you too can plant churches! Watch out, this book may change your life."

■ JR Woodward, national director of the V3 Church Planting Movement, author of *Creating a Missional Culture*

"*The Wholehearted Church Planter* is a one-of-a-kind book that blends the best of spiritual disciplines for church planting leaders with creative church planting strategies. Allan Karr and Linda Bergquist get to the heart of the matter by showing us that loving God and loving people is what creates a healthy church plant. If you want to plant a church with your whole heart, read this book!"

■ Dave Ferguson, lead pastor of Community Christian Church (with multiple sites in the Chicago area), coauthor of *On the Verge*

BOOKS BY
The Columbia Partnership Ministry Colleagues

George W. Bullard Jr.
Every Congregation Needs a Little Conflict

FaithSoaring Churches
Pursuing the Full Kingdom Potential of Your Congregation

Richard L. Hamm
Recreating the Church

Edward H. Hammett
Making Shifts without Making Waves:
A Coach Approach to Soulful Leadership

Reaching People under 40 while Keeping People over 60:
Being Church to All Generations

Spiritual Leadership in a Secular Age: Building
Bridges Instead of Barriers

Key Leadership Books

Gregory L. Hunt
Leading Congregations through Crisis

Cynthia Woolever and Deborah Bruce
Leadership That Fits Your Church:
What Kind of Pastor for What Kind of Congregation

The Sustaining Pastoral Excellence Peer Learning Team
So Much Better: How Thousands of Pastors Help Each Other Thrive

Larry McSwain
The Calling of Congregational Leadership:
Being, Knowing and Doing Ministry

For more leadership resources, see
TheColumbiaPartnership.org
ChalicePress.com

The Wholehearted CHURCH PLANTER
Leadership from the Inside Out

Allan Karr and Linda Bergquist
Foreword by J.D. Payne

CHALICE
PRESS

ST. LOUIS, MISSOURI

Readers should be aware that Internet websites offered as citations and/or sources of further information may have changed or disappeared between the time this was written and when it was read.

Cover art: Shutterstock and iStock.
Cover design: Scribe, Inc.
Interior design: Crystal Devine

Visit www.chalicepress.com.

Print: 9780827243026   EPUB: 9780827243033   EPDF: 9780827243040

Library of Congress Cataloging-in-Publication Data available upon request.

To Eric, the love of my life,
who helps me to think, be, and act
in more whole ways. Linda

To my partners in life and ministry:
To Kathy, my beloved wife;
To Kenny, my mentor and friend;
To all my children. Thanks, Allan

Contents

Editor's Foreword

Inspiration and Wisdom for Twenty-First-Century Christian Leaders

You have chosen wisely in deciding to study and learn from a book published in The Columbia Partnership Leadership Series with Chalice Press. We publish for

- Congregational leaders who desire to serve with greater faithfulness, effectiveness, and innovation.
- Christian ministers who seek to pursue and sustain excellence in ministry service.
- Members of congregations who desire to reach their full kingdom potential.
- Christian leaders who desire to use a coach approach in their ministry.
- Denominational and parachurch leaders who want to come alongside affiliated congregations in a servant leadership role.
- Consultants and coaches who desire to increase their learning concerning the congregations and Christian leaders they serve.

The Columbia Partnership Leadership Series is an inspiration- and wisdom-sharing vehicle of The Columbia Partnership, a community of Christian leaders who are seeking to transform the capacity of the North American church to pursue and sustain vital Christ-centered ministry. You can connect with us at www.TheColumbiaPartnership.org.

Primarily serving congregations, denominations, educational institutions, leadership development programs, and parachurch organizations, the Partnership also seeks to connect with individuals, businesses, and other organizations seeking a Christ-centered spiritual focus.

We welcome your comments on these books, and we welcome your suggestions for new subject areas and authors we ought to consider.

The Columbia Partnership
332 Valley Springs Road, Columbia, SC 29223-6934
Voice: 803.622.0923, www.TheColumbiaPartnership.org

Acknowledgments

Linda:

This book contains the stories of dozens of church planters, many of whom have challenged, taught, blessed, amazed, entreated, drilled, polished, and edified me over the last thirty years. These friends, plus countless others whose stories do not appear here, are my heroes. Their prayers are my prayers, and their stories are mine, too. Their failures are my failures, but their victories belong to them, and, most importantly, to the Father. Thank you, church planters, for your dedication, your courage, your vulnerability, and your faith.

I would also like to acknowledge my associate, Brook Ewbank, who took on many extra tasks that in turn allowed me to submit this book to our publishers on time. Thank you, Brook, for writing newsletters, mentoring planters, assessing church planter candidates, organizing projects, teaching at the prison, and so many other things you do that allowed me to co-author this book.

Reta Beall, you are an awesome editor. The technical aspects of writing are so tedious for me. You made my chapters better not only because of your expertise in grammar and punctuation, but also because you ask challenging questions. You hung with me until the end.

My friend and co-author, Allan, I love and appreciate you so very much. It has been great to write our second book together. We think in unison about so many things that matter. We also bring such different stories and perspectives. I can't even imagine writing this book without you.

Kristina Bergquist, when a daughter comes home from college for the summer, she should get spoiled. Is that not what mothers are for? Instead, I holed up for a few weeks. You even pulled together my bibliography from a large box of what must seem like very odd books. Thank you for your diligence and thoughtfulness.

Finally, thank you, Eric Bergquist, for all of the wisdom and creativity you have extended to me in the process of writing this book. You have been generous with your own ideas, and also with your honest and open critique. I appreciate the perfect cups of decaf you brewed for me so I could write in the early mornings. Thanks for your patience with me during those insane hours when I tried to hide my computer's light under the covers while I punched out just a few more paragraphs. I didn't do a very good job as a stealth author, did I? You are incredibly patient. Thank you!

Allan:

I would first like to acknowledge my wife, Kathy Karr. We have shared over twenty-seven years of life and ministry. This book is based on the experiences our journey has provided. Kathy contributed the bulk of the practical advice of chapter 9. A wise and caring person, she has always been a faithful ministry partner and devoted mom for our children. I can use her life as an example of wholeheartedness. I always say, "If you know my wife Kathy, you will like us."

Second, I really want to acknowledge my children. My children make my life rich. Four of my children have spent their whole lives with us and have been travel companions on many of our adventures. Many of the stories in this book they have experienced firsthand. My two other children came to us later their lives and have given much joy as God constantly reminds of His love and faithfulness. Their lives are also part of this story. Some adults have adopted us, so that we have become their family. I am very proud of all my children. Their lives inspire me. I cannot tell you how much I value my family.

Next, I would like to acknowledge the contribution to my life of my friend Kenny Moore. He contributed material in many places in this book, but especially chapter 16. As a mentor, he has been invaluable in helping me learn more about missiology, grace, and the Holy Spirit. I am always very aware of how much he has influenced me. I also appreciate his constant prayers as a daily reminder of all the things that are already true in union with Christ.

My co-author Linda Bergquist has a beautiful mind and always encourages me and everyone else around her. She has forgotten more ideas than most people have ever had in the first place. This is our second book together, and it has left us better friends than when we started again. Thanks for the teamship!

Many other people are part of my stories. I have been a pastor and church planter for decades, so it is impossible to mention each person individually. I am completely aware that my ideas and who I am as a person today are a mosaic of many who have influenced me and shared my journey. I acknowledge their impact in my life and the material of this book.

Finally, I would like to acknowledge the community of faith I share in my church. In 2013, Ethne Church Network celebrates eleven years together as a church. The value of this Christian family cannot be overstated. All my children have benefited from the loving nurture of this community. They have loyally prayed and supported all the ministry adventures and risks we have taken. They were often traveling companions as we explored the faraway places of the Kingdom.

Foreword

We have lived in the world of the "instant" for a long period of time. Though microwave ovens preceded my birth, I can remember my first remote control television–no more wasting time walking across the room. Fast-food chains were up and running long before I was around, but I can remember when my hometown got a pizza restaurant that would provide our order in thirty minutes or less. I found it fascinating when we could leave the house, miss our favorite television program, only to return and have it recorded on a VHS tape available to watch anytime we desired. At present many people have on-demand movies and television. Social media continue to add fuel to the fire of instant desire.

Unfortunately, this demand for the instant has influenced the world of church planters to an unhealthy degree. We want to know "how" to do something, and we want to know it now. To produce the desired results, we are sometimes quick to take for granted the extremely important elements that are not novel. Such is a recipe for disaster in the Kingdom.

While in a hurry to hang a ceiling fan in my kitchen, I skimmed the instructions and quickly got the item in place. I was very excited to see that once I turned on the electricity that the fan's lights came on and blades started spinning. However, much to my anger and surprise, the fan came crashing to the floor when I pulled on the chain to turn it off! Everything looked great on the outside. But I had failed to put three small screws in place. In my desire to have the finished product–the installation of a ceiling fan–I overlooked three key components!

What you have in this book is not an instant how-to manual. You will not find information on the latest and greatest church planting methodology. There is no step-by-step guide here describing how to plant a church. For such information, you will need to look elsewhere. Rather, what you will find in the pages of this work are matters of the heart–the whole heart.

"Church planters," Allan and Linda write, "are first and foremost disciples who must know and love God, know and love people, and know and appropriately love themselves, rather than supreme vision casters or awesome orators." Well said! In a day and age when the Church is often looking for the shiniest, brightest, coolest, and hippest trend–especially in the world of church planting–Allan and Linda direct us elsewhere. They remind us that the expectations of our cultures are not always in line with the standard of the Kingdom.

In the sea of church planting literature, Allan and Linda are navigating waters that everyone knows about, but few authors are traveling. In America today we are quick to move to and fro throughout the world, looking for the magic method to plant a church. And yet, while in the process, there is a still, small voice reminding us of the fundamentals; oftentimes we are guilty of neglecting that ancient whisper and losing our first love. And later, after many shipwrecks, we realize that maybe, just maybe, missionaries should be concerned with the matters of the heart *first*, and then mechanics later. This book is written to help us avoid such disasters.

But before someone is quick to write off this book as one composed by conductors who are good at telling others how to play an instrument but have never picked up one themselves, he or she should understand that these authors have years of experience in planting churches. They are not only experienced missionaries, but also seasoned trainers—with years of assisting others on the church planting journey. So, for them to write a book about the importance of loving God, other believers, self, and those outside the Kingdom, it would be worth our time to consider their words before departing for the task of church planting.

For a decade, I had the privilege of serving with Allan as part of the same missions agency. Twice a year we would gather somewhere in the U.S. or Canada for our annual agency meetings. We have shared many meals, cups of coffee/tea, and stories. He has a heart for the nations and for equipping and mobilizing others for such Kingdom work. His life contains many sacrifices to make this happen.

For example, I remember shortly after beginning my ministry role ten years ago that my supervisor sent me to Denver to spend a weekend with Allan at a training event he was leading. I was greatly looking forward to this time and to seeing what the Lord had been doing in Colorado—for I had heard many wonderful stories of church planting activities in that state.

After arriving at my hotel, I called Allan only to discover that he was scheduled for outpatient surgery the next day. He had hurt his arm. Though in forty-eight hours he was supposed to be leading a church planters' training conference, he was not fazed. And sure enough, two days later, he was training church planters at the Ponderosa camp near Larkspur, Colorado, while in much pain, reclining in a La-Z-Boy chair, and arm in a sling! Such was one of my early memories of Allan's heart for equipping church planters, even with much discomfort to himself!

Interestingly, I met Linda at that same camp, though sometime later at another church planters' training event. I had heard of some of the great things the Lord was doing through her service in the San Francisco area. Over the course of a few days, I was able to get to know her and her heart for the multiplication of disciples and churches, especially in urban contexts.

As you read through this book, I want to encourage you to examine your heart. Ask the Lord of the Harvest to prepare you for the harvest field. But be warned. Such is not a safe prayer to pray, for the development of a wholehearted church planter requires the scalpel of the Great Heart Surgeon. We may have the outstanding missionary zeal, but zeal without knowledge is not good (Prov. 19:2). We may have great faith and make great sacrifices to be church planters, but without love we are nothing (1 Cor. 13). Allan and Linda remind us of the importance of the right knowledge and love. Learn from the experiences of the authors, even when you disagree with them. I pray that through the pages of this work you will become more like Jesus and better prepared to take the gospel to the nations!

J. D. Payne
Pastor of Church Multiplication,
The Church at Brook Hills, Birmingham, Alabama,
Author of *Discovering Church Planting*

Preface

The Wholehearted Church Planter

The intent of this book is to at once both expand and tighten the gates that serve to permit or deny access into the church planting arena. Our premise is that almost anyone can plant *some* kind of church, whether large or small, cross-cultural or same-culture, organism-like or with sophisticated organization. A theological rather than a cultural definition of *church* is necessary to substantiate this claim. Church planting is not about buildings, budgets, or number of congregants; it is about Jesus-following communities of any size or kind. Linda and Allan have observed churches of various sizes structured in many different ways that were started by all kinds of people with a wide variety of spiritual gifts, experiences, strengths, and weaknesses. If we are truthful about it, we already realize that almost nobody can plant every kind of church.

Theologically, three things define a church: (1) the worshiping people of God, (2) the gathered community of God, (3) the sent people of God. With Christ as its center, the Church's response to the Father is worship. Individual worship is appropriate and compelling, but private worship is not an expression of the corporate peoplehood of Christ's followers. The Church worships as the gathered community of God, the *koinonia*. A church is a real community that offers nurture and nourishment as it practices "one-anothering." One-anothering must reach beyond the local, gathered community. Scripture points to the Church as the *apostolos*, or the sent people of God. As the Father sent the Son, the Son sends out His disciples in His name and in the power of the Holy Spirit. Churches do not always begin with these three things in place, but it is critical that, over time, they experience growth in all three areas.

The "who" aspect of our assertion that almost anyone can start a church does not include far-fetched examples, such as, "What about a 110-year-old person on life support or the very young child?" You get the idea. It is also important to differentiate between starting/catalyzing/initiating a church and leading/pastoring/shepherding that church over time. Some individuals take on shepherding roles and stay with churches to grow them. Other men and women start churches they never intend to lead. Allan, for example, has both started churches and led them over time. Linda, on the other hand, is a serial church planter who catalyzes new churches over and over again but never stays long with any. Allan has a preference for stories, and Linda loves concepts. You will see both our differences and our similarities as you read this book. Because we bring different gifts, capacities, preferences, and perspectives to the table, we decided to put our individual names to each chapter so readers would know whose voice they are hearing.

The underlying qualification for church planting as presented here is *wholeheartedness*, a far more demanding criterion than skill level or even spiritual giftedness. The biblical challenge to wholeheartedness is the Great Commandment: "Thou shalt love the Lord thy God with thy whole heart, and with thy whole soul, and with all thy strength, and with all thy mind: and thy neighbour as thyself" (Lk. 10:27, Douay-Rheims Bible). Church planters are first and foremost disciples who must know and love God, know and love people, and know and appropriately love themselves, rather than supreme vision casters or awesome orators. We are calling this the "Luke 10:27 call." We are also making an assumption that wholehearted church planters do not work alone. They work with family, team members, partner churches, and other traveling companions. Church planting works best when the broad community that gathers around a new church also loves and knows God, people, and self. This volume is written for them, too, because these aspects of *one* Great Commandment represent elemental truths for *every* Christian.

The first section of this book addresses knowing God, which is quite different from knowing *about* God, and loving Him in tangible ways. Loving Him is the commandment upon which everything else is contingent. For all Christians, not just Christian leaders, knowing God means being swept into the beauty of His presence—a personal call to worship: "While they were worshiping the Lord and fasting, the Holy Spirit said, 'Set apart for me Barnabas and Saul for the [church planting] work to which I have called them" (Acts 13:2).

Understanding God's nature (within human limits) and knowing the implications that stem from who He is are critical capacities. Knowing and loving God means acknowledging His mission, purposes, and activities. Knowing and loving God means embracing Him as a relational God who is relational inside of His very own being. God is a relational Trinity. All three aspects of His Person are fully active and engaged in every missional act. To love God means choosing to imitate His Person, obey His commandments, and embrace His mission. The main role of a church planter is to multiply Jesus' DNA into the lives of others and to form new faith communities out of these "Jesus DNA bearers."

Sections two and three of this book are about knowing and loving people. We divided *knowing* and *loving* here mostly for readability. If the two sections were written as one, it would be too lengthy. However, the twin concepts of knowing and loving are as difficult to separate in this section as they are in the rest of this book. The reason we have so much to say here is that knowing and loving people is the day-to-day work of church planting. Knowing and loving is also the arena in which church planters most frequently ask for help. The people we are talking about are communities of people who share some kind of common identity, such as geographical or familial ties. They are a people God has called all of us to love as neighbors and as ourselves. Sometimes they are men, women, and children with whom we share common heritage, customs, values, and worldviews. Sometimes we are quite different from the specific people God has given to us for spiritual safekeeping.

How will we come to know them, and how will we go about learning to love them? The chapters in these two sections will cover approaches to knowing all kinds of people who live in apartment complexes, neighborhoods, towns, suburbs, or cities. How can various approaches and tools help us? How will we learn to love them? We learn to love only by actively blessing, respecting, honoring, and serving them while helping them come to multiply Jesus' DNA. What can we learn from knowing and loving both ordinary and extraordinary people that will help us to be better and more wholehearted church planters?

Section four is about knowing and loving self in healthy, biblical ways. In our experience, people leave themselves out of the equation when they consider how, where, why, and when they will plant churches. Part of the problem is a model-driven approach that predetermines a planter's set of skills, experiences, and spiritual gifts. The problem is that while models present helpful ways to imagine and are great places from which to glean good ideas, no one model is the best use of every church planter's capacities. Augustine once said, "People travel to wonder at the height of mountains, at the huge waves of the sea, at the long courses of rivers, at the vast compass of the ocean, at the circular motion of the stars; and they pass by themselves without wondering."[1]

To overlook the uniquely created person God has formed each church planter to be is neither biblical nor wise. We began with the claim that almost everyone who embodies three critical capacities has the ability to start *some* kind of church. At the same time, this means that not every person can start every kind of church. Apparently, this is quite all right with God, who did not choose cloning as His process for creating the world. At the same time, it is possible to make some general assumptions about individuals with certain kinds of talents and gift mixes. For example, individuals with primary pastoral gifts start churches differently than apostolically gifted people. The challenge is listening in humility to God's calling and to what He says.

Knowing and loving God, people, and self are not necessarily sophisticated competencies. Allan and Linda both teach church planting to seminary students. At the same time, Allan plants churches among new

xx   *The Wholehearted Church Planter*

refugees, and Linda teaches church planting classes in a prison. In both refugee situations and in prisons, some individuals are actually functionally illiterate. Two of Jesus' closest disciples were illiterate, but they still managed to find ways to pass down the eternal Word of God. "When they saw the courage of Peter and John and realized that they were unschooled, ordinary men, they were astonished and they took note that these men had been with Jesus" (Acts 4:13). This book was written to help church planters and to help people who help church planters. We offer it believing that every follower of Christ has a precious church planting kernel within.

Chapter 1

A Wholehearted Relationship with the Father

LINDA BERGQUIST

Let thy desire be the vision of God, thy fear the loss of Him, thy sorrow His absence, and thy joy in that which may take thee to Him; and thy life shall be in great peace. —TERESA OF AVILA

Patrick, patron saint of Ireland, is recalled as one of history's most devoted followers of Jesus and as an exceptionally prolific church planter. He was kidnapped at age sixteen and forced into slave labor as a shepherd. Stripped of everything but his faith, he turned to God. Patrick wrote, "I used to pasture the flock each day, and I used to pray many times a day. More and more did the love of God, and my fear of him and faith increase, and my spirit was moved so that in a day [I said] from one up to a hundred prayers, and in the night a like number."[1]

After many years in slavery, Patrick escaped miraculously. After he returned home, the Spirit of God compelled him to return to the land of his captivity and offer God's love to a people he could have easily hated. He said that he "found it a privilege...that the Lord should grant his humble servant this, that after hardships and such great trials, after captivity, after many years, he should give me so much favour with these people."[2] Patrick subsequently evangelized over one hundred thousand pagans and started two hundred churches. He was a church planter who wholeheartedly loved God and the people to whom he was sent.

God is looking for wholehearted disciples to represent His Kingdom in this age. They are the choicest DNA carriers for the kind of churches that He wants to multiply. The process begins with the Great Commandment given in Luke 10:27: "'Love the Lord your God with all your heart

1

and with all your soul and with all your strength and with all your mind'; and, 'Love your neighbor as yourself.'" The first and greatest commandment, plus Jesus' complementary call to love others as one's self, is the core criterion for walking with God, helping others to be disciples, and starting churches.

This has everything to do with God working through the church planter's character. Nothing else can substitute—not beautifully crafted vision statements, great business plans, well-defined core values, talented team members, or even a seminary degree. The premise of this book, then, is that almost anyone who is truly faithful to the Great Commandment as given by Christ can plant some kind of church. It does not mean that everyone *should* plant a church—God calls *some* as apostles. Others, and again *not all*, are pastors, teachers, and so forth. We simply mean that all kinds of individuals who wholeheartedly know and love God, know and love people, and appropriately know and love self make the best church planters.

The phrase "can plant some kind of church" requires some definition. An example from the San Francisco Bay Area helps explain it. A few years ago, some missionaries and strategists living there shifted their church planting priorities. After years of research and observation, they discerned four primary ways they saw God working to seed the area with new churches: (1) The Antioch Priority—developing strong, sending base churches; (2) The Acts 2 Priority—multiplying indigenous missional communities; (3) The Athens Priority—starting churches among least-reached peoples; and (4) The Amos Priority—planting churches by engaging the gospel in ministries of justice. Naturally, any of these approaches can be combined with any another. Each of the four is celebrated, resourced, and evaluated within its own genre, and church planters' leadership capacities are assessed according to whichever strategy they are called to use. This means that a wide range of equally passionate, but differently called and gifted individuals can engage in church planting. Few people can start every kind of church, but given the Great Commandment, most people can start some kind of church.

Linda's Journey

Just one week after I committed my life to Christ, I took my first mission trip—an exploratory trip to an Apache reservation in preparation for a summer venture a few months later. Unexpectedly, I became involved in planting a church in another part of the reservation that needed a church. I was even asked to lead the initial project. On my return home, my church asked me to help them start a new church a few miles a way. On my way to seminary two years later, I asked my pastor's advice on where to plug into a congregation while in school. He suggested a church near seminary where I could work in their house church ministry on Sunday mornings and attend the larger congregation in the evenings. When I arrived at seminary, I immediately joined a house church that had a pastor, but no other members. I helped catalyze that effort as a co-planter, and it grew into a healthy house church.

A year and a half later, while knocking on doors in the neighborhood, I met a Cambodian family. They invited me in, and a friendship began. The next Sunday, while I was visiting another church, that family, plus fifty other Cambodians, showed up. It turned out that they were Christians, and they wanted to become a church. When the pastor discovered that I knew the group's leader and that I had experience starting a church, he asked me to stay and lead the project. When I returned home after seminary, one family sent their daughter with me to help start a Cambodian church there. We quickly started a ministry, and it grew enough that it soon needed a pastor who would stay with the congregation while I became involved in starting more new churches. These early experiences, all before I really knew much about church planting, shaped my belief that church planting does not require much experience, or even a mature Christian leader.

Yea-sayers and Naysayers

If our claim is valid, it will relieve and release some people, and, conversely, it will be a bit bothersome to others. Some who are most likely to agree with us include the following:

- Church planters who want to live more fully in the midst of a hundred tasks
- Church leaders who yearn to spawn many indigenous planters from their churches
- Missionary types who plant slowly and faithfully among least-reached peoples
- Pastors who see church-starting potential in their parishes, but need encouragement
- Less experienced individuals who prefer to start small as they learn new skills
- Bivocational planters who hope to reproduce more manageable-sized churches
- Postmodern pilgrims who realize that different ways of leading are emerging
- Missional leaders who dream of rapid, lay-led, indigenous church multiplication
- Potential planters with extraordinary relational capacity, but lesser oratory ability
- Churches that choose to plant churches in frontier settings, including overseas.

Others will disagree with our claim. They will most likely do so out of either a less inclusive criteria for defining church, a set of experiences that shapes their understanding of leadership, or a different commitment to what it means to "bear much fruit." Measuring fruit may be the single greatest obstacle for skeptics. Hosea taught that fruitfulness is sometimes a selfish, rather than a Kingdom, endeavor:

> Israel was a spreading vine;
>   he brought forth fruit for himself.
> As his fruit increased,
>   he built more altars;
> as his land prospered... (Hos. 10:1)

Of Knowing God

The apostle Paul spoke to the Colossians about a different kind of fruit bearing. Calling them God's holy and faithful people (Col. 1:1), he let them know that he was praying for God to fill them "with the knowledge of his will through all the wisdom and understanding that the Spirit gives" (Col. 1:9b). He encouraged them to live their lives in a way that was pleasing to God in every way, which would not only result in the kind of fruit God wants, but also would help them increase in the knowledge of God. Knowing God was paramount to their growing even more fully into their capacity to live as a holy and faithful people (Col. 1: 9–10).

> This is what the LORD says:
> "Let not the wise boast of their wisdom or the strong boast of their strength or the rich boast of their riches, but let the one who boasts boast about this: that they have the understanding to know me, that I am the LORD, who exercises kindness, justice and righteousness on earth, for in these I delight," declares the LORD. (Jer. 9:23–24)

The word translated as *know* is *yada'* in Hebrew, and the phrase *Yada' Yahweh* means to know God relationally, fully, practically, and experientially.

Ginosko and Epignosis

Of the eight words for the verb "to know" in the New Testament, the Greek word most like *yada* is *ginosko*. It indicates a connection or deep familiarity and even a relationship between the known and the knowing ones. Sometimes it is translated as to perceive, recognize, or understand. The term is used seventy times in John and 1 John alone: "My sheep listen to my voice; I know them, and they follow me" (Jn. 10:27); "Now this is eternal life: that they may know you, the only true God, and Jesus Christ, whom you have sent" (Jn. 17:3); "Whoever does not love does not know God, because God is love" (1 Jn. 4:8); "We know that we have come to know him if we obey his commands" (1 Jn. 2:3).

Another Greek term translated "knowledge" is *epignosis*, a compound word taken from epi, which means upon or toward, plus *ginosis*. It means an even fuller kind of knowing, or a knowledge that builds upon *ginosko*. It shows up, for example, in Paul's prayer for the Colossians mentioned previously in this chapter: "...asking God to fill you with the *knowledge* of his will through all spiritual wisdom and understanding..." (1:9b), "bearing fruit in every good work, growing in the *knowledge* of God" (1:10b, emphasis added). *Yada, ginosko,* and *epignosis* are gifts from God to His people. They are traits that are wonderfully evident in the lives of good church planters.

Caleb, Wholehearted Man of the Hour

Caleb, from the tribe of Judah, was God's man for the job. A missionary, explorer, visionary, and groundbreaker for Kingdom work, Caleb walked closely with God and came to know Him well. The result of his relationship with God was that in all that he did, Caleb served God with his whole heart. God said so, Moses said so, and Caleb was not shy about calling himself wholehearted either. In one of the many instances when the wilderness-walking Israelites moaned and groaned to Moses about how God was leading them, Caleb presented a sharp contrast. Along with his teammate, Joshua, he fell to the ground, tore his clothes in grief, and begged the people to believe that the land to which God was trying to lead them was a place filled with milk and honey.

When the Israelites continued to rebel and talked about stoning Moses, Aaron, Joshua, and Caleb, God became angry with them and said that, with the exception of Joshua and Caleb, whom He rewarded, they would never see the Promised Land. God singled out Caleb and explained that because Caleb had a different spirit and followed Him wholeheartedly, God would bring Caleb into the land and would give it to his descendants (Num. 14:24). Moses repeated the story several times, reminding the Israelites of Caleb's wholeheartedness (Num. 32:11–12; Deut. 1:36). Caleb himself repeated these same words (Josh. 14:8–9).

Wholehearted Living

Time after time in the wilderness, the Israelites showed that their hearts were not whole, but divided. They continually complained to God, built idols, and worshiped them. Christians learn to become wholehearted followers of Christ by spending time seeking God in His Word. Scripture teaches that the Word of God is alive, active, and sharper than any double-edged sword. This sword cuts away that which is divided and unholy with laser-like sharpness. It "penetrates even to dividing soul and spirit, joints and marrow; it judges the thoughts and attitudes of the heart" (Heb. 4:12). The Spirit of God seeks church planters whose devotional patterns allow for God to purify their lives, for only the pure in heart have the capacity to see Him and to reflect Him back to others (Mt. 5:8).

On the day of his ordination, A.W. Tozer wrote out a prayer to God. Many years later it was published as *For Pastors Only*:

> Save me from the curse that lies dark across the face of the modern clergy, the curse of compromise, of imitation, of professionalism. Save me from the error of judging a church by its size, its popularity, or the amount of its yearly offering. Help me to remember that I am a prophet; not a promoter, not a religious manager—but a prophet. Let me never become a slave to crowds. Heal my soul of carnal ambitions, and deliver me from the itch for publicity.[3]

Tozer was writing about pastors with divided hearts and was asking God to keep his heart whole and true for the duration of his ministry.

Brother Lawrence of the Resurrection (1614 –1691) worked as a lay brother in a Catholic monastery in Paris. He did not have enough schooling to qualify as a priest, so he simply lived in the monastery and served in the kitchen. Nevertheless, his contemporaries knew him as a man who knew and loved God. His writings, compiled as *The Practice of the Presence of God*, became a well-known Christian classic. He wrote, "Before we can love, we must know. We must know someone before we can love him. How shall we keep our 'first love' for the Lord? By constantly knowing Him better! Then how shall we know the Lord? We must often turn to Him, think of Him, behold Him. Then our heart will be found with our treasure."[4] This is how Brother Lawrence made the connection between knowing God and loving Him.

Wanted: Holy Men and Women

In 2005–2006, the Francis Schaeffer Institute interviewed 1,050 Evangelical and Reformed pastors. Their survey showed that 72 percent of them only studied the Bible when they were preparing for sermons or lessons and that only 26 percent said they regularly had personal devotions and felt they were adequately fed spiritually.[5] Other casualties were presented in this survey as well. For example, 30 percent of the pastors admitted they had either been involved in "an ongoing affair or a one-time sexual encounter with a parishioner." Seventy-one percent claimed they were "burned out, and they battle depression beyond fatigue on a weekly and even a daily basis." Is there any correlation between these statistics and the fact that a whopping 72 percent spent time in the Bible only when engaged in sermon preparation while just 26 percent had regular personal devotions? Only through devotional time with God in His Word do Christians come to know, love, and obey Him.

Seven years before the writing of this book, I (Linda) traveled with my family to India. The concept of the holy person came to life in that country, which, in many regions, is more spiritual than secular. We spent a week traveling throughout the state of Rajasthan and finally arrived at the magnificent city of Jaisalmer. After we checked into a hotel, my husband and daughter left to go camelback riding, while I ventured into the town to check out the marketplace that had seemed to hum with excitement when we had passed through it earlier. However, by the time I arrived, the streets were empty. As I stood puzzled at the sudden quiet, a crowd of brightly dressed women and children appeared singing and dancing down the street. They beckoned me to follow. I held back, not at all sure where this parade would take me. Soon a taxi drove by. I asked the driver about what I had seen. He said that a holy man had just arrived in town. He had walked barefoot all the way from the Ganges, bringing holy water from the river and stories to share. The whole town showed up for the event.

As we traveled through India, we found that the role of the holy man persisted in other places as well. How could the role of India's Hindu holy men remain so spiritually vital in comparison to the increasingly secularized role of the pastor or priest in the West? Who will model holiness in ways that facilitate church planters being raised up as holy people?

How Church Planters Inadvertently Nurture Divided Hearts

In 1987, just about the time when some of today's church planters were born, Eugene Peterson observed, "The pastors of America have metamorphosed into a company of shopkeepers, and the shops they keep are churches. They are preoccupied with shopkeeper's concerns—how to keep the customers happy, how to lure customers away from competitors down the street, how to package the goods so that customers will lay out more money."[6] Was Peterson correct? Is his commentary more accurate or less accurate today than it was in 1987?

It is fully possible to be a businessperson and a holy person at once. In fact, the world needs more sanctified business people, many of whom are called to start and lead churches. Peterson's point is that business practices should not govern churches. Instead, Kingdom practices must be reflected in the business practices of Christians (Lk. 12:34). John MacArthur agrees, "The church must realize that its mission has never been public relations or sales; we are called to live holy lives and declare God's raw truth—lovingly but uncompromisingly—to an unbelieving world."[7]

One new trend in the Christian world is the emergence of microbusinesses that support sustainable causes, support workplace ministers, and bring Kingdom values into the workplace. In a recent conversation, Linda's friend Andrew Jones spoke about Christian entrepreneurs in Europe who are using the Bible to teach business principles and run microbusinesses. Instead of business practices infiltrating the church, leaders are opting for faith principles that infiltrate business. They are conducting business meetings that apply biblical principles.

What Stands in the Way?

So many diversions get in the way of a church planter's quest for holiness:

1. *Time Pressures.* Real and perceived time pressures can push even an earnest individual into unhealthy patterns, such as spurious devotional time and irregular Sabbath keeping. Holiness is pursued in relationship to quality time with God.

2. *Embracing Secular Leadership Styles.* God's way is servant leadership, but some people choose leadership styles that position them as rulers rather than as servants. They rely on second tier sources of power and influence, such as position and money, rather than on spiritual and relational sources of authority.

3. *Imitating Others.* We easily fall prey to the temptation of imitating other church planters (especially successful ones) instead of allowing God to shape us. Learning from others is good, but it can also be a diversion from what God intends.

4. *A Competitive Spirit.* Church planters are wired for adventure. Many are driven to succeed. however, we have no good reason to set ourselves up in a competitive relationship with the church down the street or the church plant across town.

5. *An Obsession with Measuring Everything.* Church planters are sometimes fooled into thinking that things such as members, conversions, and baptisms are indications of God's favor or of the church planter's worth. However, "Not everything that can be counted counts, and not everything that counts can be counted."[8]

6. *Money Matters.* Jesus taught, "No one can serve two masters. Either he will hate the one and love the other, or he will be devoted to the one and despise the other. You cannot serve both God and Money" (Mt. 6:24). Church planters sometimes feel forced into decisions based on financial tensions rather than on obedience to God and to the vision He gave them. Wherever their treasure is, the heart follows.

Saying Yes to God

At the 2011 Radicalis Conference for young leaders, pastor/author Rick Warren asked church leaders to begin radically representing Jesus by saying "yes" to God in all aspects of their lives before asking others to do the same. The theme of this conference was God's radical love for people and the appropriate "yes" response of those who are caught up in His love.[9] What does it mean to voice a wholehearted "yes" to God, including His will and way, His mission, and His Kingdom? What is it about church planting out of a thankful, yes-filled heart that is so rare, so essential, and so magnetic?

The world is desperate for leaders who have wholehearted Jesus DNA and transmit it through their words and actions to next-generation leaders. The mission of God cannot afford to depend on the organizational exclusivity that has characterized church planting in the West for the last few generations. Sometimes, wholehearted leaders, such as those addressed in this chapter, will start churches as well-structured church organizations, but not every one of them should do so. On the other hand, leaders who excel organizationally but do not carry wholehearted DNA sometimes start well-structured churches. Linda and Allan wish that this never happened. This book aims to stimulate and release church planting by focusing on the priorities of the Great Commandment

Chapter 2

To Love a Greathearted God

LINDA BERGQUIST

...whoever practices and teaches these commands will be called great in the kingdom of heaven. –Jesus (in Matthew 5:19)

What does the term *greathearted* mean to you? The term is not a familiar one, perhaps because this quality is such a rare trait. The closest synonyms are generous, benevolent, and magnanimous; but none of these terms begins to approximate the full meaning of the word. The term *greathearted* evokes a sense of nobility, of sacrifice, and a way of treating others with radical fairness and justice, even when they do not deserve to be treated well. Greatheartedness describes God's character and is also characteristic of people who know and love Him with all their hearts.

God Is Great and He Is Good

Reflect on a few verses from Psalm 145 that begin to declare His greatheartedness:

> Your kingdom is an everlasting kingdom,
>   and your dominion endures through all generations.
> The Lord is trustworthy in all he promises
>   and faithful in all he does.
> The Lord upholds all who fall
>   and lifts up all who are bowed down.
> The eyes of all look to you,
>   and you give them their food at the proper time.
> You open your hand
>   and satisfy the desires of every living thing. (Ps. 145:13–16)

God's benevolent grace is offered to all creation—all living things—and not just humans. God's benevolent grace is expansive, inclusive, and extravagant. *The Message* translates verse 16 like this: "Generous to a fault, / you lavish your favor on all creatures."

Who can know this God and not worship Him?

Five verses earlier in Psalm 145:8, the psalmist declares, "The LORD is gracious and compassionate, / slow to anger and rich in love." These words appear over and over again in the Old Testament. Each mention is a reference to Exodus 34 as part of the story of the wilderness wanderings mentioned in chapter one of this book. Moses left the Israelites camped at the bottom of Mount Sinai while he climbed to the top to hear from God. During the forty days and nights during which Moses was away, the Lord talked with him about matters such as consecrating priests, building the Ark of the Covenant, and taking a census. At this time God gave Moses the Ten Commandments.

Moses was away so long that the people he led became afraid that he would never return, and they regressed to idol worship. God was, of course, angry (after all, he had just written in stone, "You shall have no other Gods before me," and, "You shall not make for yourself an idol"). Moses was angry, too. Moses went back up the mountain to covenant with God, and

> [T]he Lord came down in the cloud and stood there with him and proclaimed his name, the LORD. And he passed in front of Moses, proclaiming, "The LORD, the LORD, the compassionate and gracious God, slow to anger, abounding in love and faithfulness, maintaining love to thousands, and forgiving wickedness, rebellion and sin. Yet he does not leave the guilty unpunished; he punishes the children and their children for the sin of the parents to the third and fourth generation." (Ex. 34:5–7)

The Jews call these scriptures the Thirteen Attributes of God. They recite or sing them on Yom Kippur, Rosh Hashanah, Sukkot, and other high holy days as manifestations of God's presence and as a call to imitate God's character. The reluctant prophet Jonah used these words, too, remembering God's mercy, but wishing that God were not quite so patient towards everyone: "I knew that you are a gracious and compassionate God, slow to anger and abounding in love, a God who relents from sending calamity. Now, Lord, take away my life, for it is better for me to die than to live" (Jon. 4:2b–3). Describing the Day of the Lord, the prophet Joel called out for the people to repent with all their hearts and to return to God. He reminded the Israelites of God's compassion and mercy, declaring that the Lord is slow to anger and abounding in love (Joel 2:12–13).[1] God's greateartedness shows up repeatedly in Scripture through His magnanimous forgiveness, generous grace, and bountiful provision.

Greatheartedness and the Mission of God

In the beginning when God created the good earth, he put all kinds of patterns in place that he never intended to be broken, Before any language included words such as *sin, forgiveness,* and *redemption,* the Word, Jesus who was God and who was with God, participated in the world's creation. The Savior was there before the world ever needed saving. God's character was whole and complete before the fall–before anything was broken and in need of fixing and before sending was ever needed. Another way of saying this is that God's character is not dependent on our human fall.

Sometimes God is referred to as a missionary God because He is a God who sends. He sent His Son, and the Son sends His disciples to the whole world. However, sending is not the activity that makes God missional. He is missional and sends because of *who He is.* He is loving and just, generous, merciful, and holy. How could God, whose very nature is Love, *not* reach out to make it possible for those He loves to live with Him forever? How could a merciful, compassionate, and holy Creator whose nature and being are One *not* mediate an escape from human sin and help humanity find a way to live whole and above it? Would a greathearted God be any less than heroic when saving is so needed by the world?

Jesus and the Heroic Side of Greatheartedness

Woven into the concept of greatheartedness is the idea of a heroic person who saves, protects, transforms, releases, mediates, heals, and gives people hope. That's what heroes do. Some of the world's hero stories are tales of capricious individuals who are not carriers of any real greathearted attributes. Examples include pirates or various mythological gods and goddesses. In other stories, heroic acts may be what first calls attention to the greatheartedness of an individual. Jesus is the supra-hero (a hero above all heroes) who fills all of the hero roles. He alone saves, protects, transforms, releases, mediates, and heals. "In his name the nations will put their hope" (Mt. 12:21). Yet this heroic One sacrificed everything and suffered as an outcast, a man of sorrows, who was humiliated, shunned, and rejected.

The span of God's heroic, saving activity is daunting. The Father sent the Son to "save the world through him" (Jn. 3:17). Jesus "will draw all people" to himself (Jn. 12:32). He came "to save" the world (Jn. 12:47). "For God was pleased to have all his fullness dwell in him, and through him to reconcile to himself all things, whether things on earth or things in heaven, by making peace through his blood, shed on the cross" (Col. 1:19–20). Christ Jesus "gave himself as a ransom for all people" (1 Tim. 2:6b). He is the atoning sacrifice for our sins, and not only for ours but also for the sins of the whole world (1 Jn. 2:2).

God, in His generous love for the world, sent His own Son to save it. Out of obedience and compassion, Jesus transformed lives, healed the sick, gave sight to the blind, and helped the lame to walk again. He also offered release to those who were captive to sin. "Through Christ Jesus the law of the Spirit who gives life has set you free from the law of sin and death" (Rom. 8:2). Jesus proclaimed that He was sent to proclaim freedom for the prisoners and recovery of sight for the blind, to set the oppressed free (Lk. 4:18b). These things are possible in that "the Lord is the Spirit, and where the Spirit of the Lord is, there is freedom" (2 Cor. 3:17). Additionally, Christ serves as the high priest who mediates a new covenant "that those who are called may receive the promised eternal inheritance—now that he has died as a ransom to set them free from the sins committed under the first covenant" (Heb. 9:15). He is the heroic Christ.

Lessons in Greatheartedness

Greatheartedness is the yield of a life that is wholeheartedly submitted to Christ. It is worked out in obedience to him. Perhaps one reason why some missionaries are hero figures to the Christian world is that they are recognized as greathearted, too. Their selfless love for Jesus and for the world sets them apart as a somehow different kind of people. God never intended for some followers to love and obey Him more fully or serve Him more heroically than others. Greatheartedness is available to everyone. Here are a few helps for the journey.

1. Live well with Jesus. Jesus wants all His followers to become greathearted, too. In doing so, they represent God. The twelve lived and traveled with Him. They were the primary witnesses to His character for three amazing years. They listened while Jesus told stories, pointed out the faithful acts of others, and rebuked people publicly. Not all of them became greathearted, but, at the same time, nobody can become greathearted without spending significant time close to Jesus.

2. Transcend ordinary patterns of relationship. So many scripture passages point out that Jesus longed to see the character of God replicated in the lives of others. The Sermon on the Mount offers the world's most counterintuitive lessons on how to rise above human nature to transcend what is ordinary. In Luke 6:27–28, Jesus said, "Love your enemies, do good to those who hate you, bless those who curse you, and pray for those who mistreat you." He also said that "if someone slaps you on one cheek, turn to them the other also" (v. 29). He told us that if someone takes your coat, give that person your shirt as well. If anyone takes what belongs to you, do not demand it back. Act toward others as you want them to act toward you, rather than as they actually act toward you. Jesus laid out a whole new grid for life on earth.

3. Recognize what you have been given and what you have been forgiven. Once, Peter asked Jesus how many times he should continue to forgive the brother or sister who sins against him, suggesting that seven times would be a magnanimous number. Jesus replied with an extravagant amount—seventy times more than Peter's highest estimate. Then Jesus told a parable about a benevolent king and an unmerciful servant to illustrate what He meant. In the story, the

king forgave the debts of his servant who cried for mercy, but that servant turned around and choked a fellow servant, demanding that he pay back what he owed him. When the fellow servant begged, he was denied forgiveness. The king heard about this behavior and decided to punish the unmerciful servant who had the resources to be greathearted, but was not. God expects greatheartedness to beget greatheartedness (Mt. 18:23–35).

4. Be radically generous with what Christ has given you. Dozens of New Testament passages point to God's wonderful generosity in Christ:
   a. the bountiful feeding of five thousand (Lk. 9:10–17),
   b. the graciousness of the Samaritan who went out of his way to extend help to a man who was left on the side of the road to die (Lk. 10:25–37),
   c. the care He takes of creation, including even the seemingly insignificant lilies of the field (Mt. 6:25–34),
   d. the parable of the generous landowner who gave a good paycheck even to workers who had only labored in the vineyard for a few hours (Mt. 20:1–14).

5. Recalling that "every good and perfect gift is from above" (Jas. 1:17) helps God's people to live sacrificially. Money, possessions, and even life itself belong to God. This means that all generous and sacrificial giving is an act of giving back not only to God, but also through God.

6. Dwell on noble thoughts and ideas. Great thoughts lead to greatheartedness. In Philippians 4:8, the apostle Paul commends Jesus' followers: "[W]hatever is true, whatever is noble, whatever is right, whatever is pure, whatever is lovely, whatever is admirable–if anything is excellent or praiseworthy–think about such things."

7. In his book, *Good to Great in God's Eyes: 10 Practices Great Christians Have in Common*, Chip Ingram made "Thinking Great Thoughts" his first chapter. He encourages a regular habitual practice of spending time not only in God's Word, but in other places, such as in the beauty of God's creation, as a way to develop a great mind.[2]

Pitfalls

Anyone who experiments with the practice of greatheartedness will soon discover its challenges. Even writing this chapter makes it absolutely impossible to escape the adventure. Here are some things a greathearted individual (or church planter, partner, coach, or mentor) is *not*:

1. Puffed up–boastful, prideful, egotistical, or self-seeking. "'Let the one who boasts boast in the Lord.' For it is not the one who commends himself who is approved, but the one whom the Lord commends" (2 Cor. 10:17–18). Church plants are to reflect God's glory alone and not that of an individual planter or a church planting church.

2. Petty—worried about nonessentials, keeping a record of the wrong-doings of others. Most church planters are so oriented around the big picture that they are not usually petty people. Usually details are beyond them, but they can frustrate others and unknowingly bring out the petty side of others, including their partner churches.

3. Perfectionistic—seeking the approval of people instead of God. One of the sad aspects of perfectionism is that it tends to rob time from other important tasks—such as developing relationships and caring for people. "Excellence" as a church value means more than matching tablecloths or impeccable music. Church planters and their partner churches are called to walk in grace. Perfectionism can sometimes get in the way of grace.

4. Power hungry—claiming what is God's for one's self or imagining self as better than others. Philippians 2:3 is a great antidote to this temptation. Paul says, "Do nothing out of selfish ambition or vain conceit. Rather, in humility value others above yourselves." He notes that even Jesus did not grasp at what belongs to God. Leaders should not seek to be powerful, but to empower church planters, coaches, and denominational leaders.

5. Proprietary—private, exclusive, or territorial. Sometimes Christian leaders think they are overseers of some domain, such as a people group or a geography, which they believe is exclusively theirs. They are closed-minded to advice or assistance from other partners and are unwilling to concede that it takes other individuals and other churches to take the gospel to every person. This is small-hearted, not greathearted, behavior.

6. Politically correct—substituting what is right in God's eyes for what seems right to people. Insincerity undermines truth. We have no good reason for expedient integrity. Guard against insincere relationships, even for the sake of starting and growing a church. Do not expect favoritism, and do not offer it.

Who Is Greathearted?

Linda volunteers at a prison where she has the opportunity to teach church planting to inmates. Church planting criteria do not change for prisoners. They, too, must start churches by evangelizing the lost, forming new groups, and transmitting Christlike character to new followers. They must learn to live well in fishbowl-like surroundings with many other inmates and staff who are watching their lives. One day, when Linda was teaching her students about the accountability aspect of Life Transformation Groups,[3] she asked them to develop a code of accountability that would allow them to help one another live well.

Class conversation centered on ideas that applied to hands and mouth. The group came up with these phrases: openhanded, underhanded, heavy-handed, glad handing, evenhanded, and offering a hand up. They can now ask each other in passing the simple question, "How's your hand doing?" The second set of character-based questions related to the mouth. Phrases included bad mouth, foul mouth, big mouth, loud mouth, talking out of both sides of your mouth, mealy mouth, and mouth of praise. The accountability phrase became, "Watch your mouth," or, "How's your mouth." The group had actually been helping one another with accountability even before this became a topic of conversation in a church planting class. They choose to be accountable to one another as they see one another at meals, work, class, or in the yard. Together, they want to become people of character—people of the Kingdom.

Is it really possible for prisoners, some in for life, to be greathearted? How can God move through a hardcore prison population to establish His Kingdom? This same group of prisoners has adopted a mission in Africa. In one year they sent $10,000 to dig wells and provide water for a village. Many work, but their pay is measured more in pennies than in dollars per hour. They give up some of the few worldly pleasures those pennies could buy each month for the sake of doing good in the lives of people who have less. Here is what God has to say about it:

> Brothers and sisters, think of what you were when you were called. Not many of you were wise by human standards; not many were influential; not many were of noble birth. But God chose the foolish things of the world to shame the wise; God chose the weak things of the world to shame the strong. God chose the lowly things of this world and the despised things—and the things that are not—to nullify the things that are, so that no one may boast before him. (1 Cor. 1:26–29)

Ultimately, Jesus said that the greatest will be a servant and that "those who exalt themselves will be humbled, and those who humble themselves will be exalted" (Mt. 23:12). This attitude lets you become a great church planter in prison or out. This attitude lets you instill greathearted DNA into a new church or an old prison.

Chapter 3

Knowing and Following Jesus with Your Whole Heart

ALLAN KARR

Christ is not valued at all unless He is valued above all. –St. Augustine

When You Make Disciples, Church Happens

Most church planters focus on planting a church. That sounds like a logical focal point, but a holistic biblical approach reveals that is shallow at best, and poor missiology at worst. In Matthew 28 Jesus did not commission us to go and plant churches among every people group. Instead He told us to make disciples. We are not to focus on planting a church. More properly we should concentrate on making disciples. The church is the aftermath of this process!

I delight in teaching students and mentees: "When you make disciples, church happens." When you see God's Spirit open people's hearts to transformative faith so that they become new disciples, and when you help followers of Jesus grow in maturity, they will either find an existing church, or they will follow a church planter's lead and become part of a new church, a church plant. This is true in every culture and people group where the gospel has taken root. When disciples are made, church happens, and often it is a church plant.

Making Disciples Is Jesus' Strategy

In the last words before His ascension that are found in the well-known passage of Matthew 28:19–20, Jesus instructed us: Jesus instructed us to "Go," but the Greek participle is best interpreted "Go and as you are going…"[1] However, the next phrase is quite significant, "make disciples of all the nations…" The last part of that phrase is the Greek words, "*panta ta ethne*," and is commonly translated "all the nations" in many English versions of Scripture. However, that is a weak and misunderstood translation.

This translation may be heard to mean that the teaching is about geo-political national boundaries. The word *ethne* means the ethnicities, or people groups, defined by the boundaries of culture, language, history, geography, and geo-political lines. No missiologist would argue that if we had only one missionary or one missionary unit sharing the gospel with China that the one missionary unit would fulfill Jesus' command. What a preposterous idea that we would think that we only need one missionary for any one nation, as some have advocated, even if that missionary is training indigenous populations to follow the same discipleship principle. The command is to make disciples of all the "people groups," or all the ethnicities at the very least.

We are just reaching the meat of Jesus' command, the phrase "make disciples." Notice Jesus does not say, "Go and as you go *plant churches* in all the people groups..." Nor is His command limited to "...*evangelizing* all the people groups..." Jesus told us as His disciples to *make disciples.* "Make disciples" is the major verb, the imperative verb in Jesus' command.[2] The rest of Matthew 28:19–20 fleshes out that phrase. "Baptizing" and "teaching" are descriptive modifiers telling us what it means to *make disciples.* "Make disciples" implies a holistic view of this Spirit-empowered trans-formative process. It includes the process resulting in *new birth*[3] and in the public symbol that baptism represents. Baptism is part of discipleship, but it is not limited to that, because baptism is not the beginning or the end of the command.[4] Teaching disciples of Jesus to observe all the commands of Jesus is the rest of the holistic view. In many ways, the teaching starts before salvation occurs. Teaching leads to salvation and continues when the Holy Spirit and Scriptures lead a person to a moment of sharing their transformation in a public symbol, baptism.

Teaching continues infinitely into the future as a young follower of Jesus learns more and more about new life in the Kingdom of God.[5] This is the Trinity's strategy, which Jesus expressed for the Kingdom of God: *Go and as you are going in my empowerment, make disciples of all the peoples of the world...*

Knowing Comes Through Abiding in Christ

In John 15:5, Jesus gives us His memorable teaching, "I am the vine, you are the branches; he who abides in Me and I in him, he bears much fruit, for apart from Me you can do nothing"(NASB).

Not much can be said here that scholars, preachers, and teachers have not already said thousands of times while exegeting this scripture. Still, we need to emphasize this truth again and again: wholeheartedness in church planters begins with a heart that longs to abide in Christ, and wholeheart-edness results in a heart that is abiding in Him. Abiding in Christ and wholeheartedness are inextricably linked together.

Many of us are blessed to have had a Christian heritage as children. As a pre-adolescent child, I was in church every week, usually multiple times a week. We were taught to have daily devotions, sometimes called "Quiet Times." This reflected the value of the Bible being God's Word. For the wholehearted person, knowing Jesus is dependent on a lifestyle of spending personal time in His Word. This is not meant to be a legalistic chore at a certain time of day, but rather like a healthy meal when a person is hungry. Knowing Jesus comes from spending time in the Bible, in hearing His Word come alive in your heart.

In various classes at church, in summer camps, and even as a personal "Quiet Time" focus, I gave energy to memorizing verses of the Bible. Sometimes this was done to reach goals of achievement in classes and camps. Regardless of the motivation, at this mature time of my life I am so thankful that many of those verses are ingrained into my memory. I value the Word of God more and more as time passes.

Being and remaining wholehearted involves knowing passages of scripture, learning new passages and principles from Scripture, and listening to God through Scripture regularly. These daily practices remind me of what is already true and prove to be key to being and living the life Scripture reveals.

Fruitfulness in Church Planting Comes from Knowing Him

The last part of John 15:5 says if we abide in Christ, we bear much fruit. Bearing fruit could mean many things. It could mean fruit of the Spirit (Gal. 5:22–23). It could mean reaping a harvest of spiritual transformation (Lk. 10:1). It could mean success in the context of drawing a crowd. Drawing a crowd is the least biblical of these ideas, but it seems to be the preferred definition of fruitfulness for most church planters. However, *wholehearted* church planters have the perspective that fruitfulness is spiritual in nature. Spiritual fruit may be the collective idea of harvest or the individual concept of fruit of the Spirit manifested in an individual's life.

I have been a church planter for almost two decades. During that time I have been around hundreds of planters. Church planters share a private fear: the fear of failure. We live in the awareness that new churches are vulnerable and fragile in the beginning. Like a newborn calf during a cold spring, church planters are susceptible to demise from a variety of dangerous elements. We often have the definition of success given to us by a church culture that borrows more from business models than Kingdom of God standards. We count "nickels and noses" (as my wife says). The size of our congregations, the size of our buildings, and the size of our budgets tend to be our measures of success. These are not biblical standards of success. Jesus spent most of His time with twelve men, and even then focused on three of them. All of them abandoned Him after His arrest, so this was not numerical success. Jesus did talk a lot about money, but most of the time He was decrying the problems it caused. Jesus talked a lot about fruitfulness, but for Him fruitfulness was spiritual in nature and always in connection to the power of the God of the universe.

Remember the last phrase of John 15:5. Jesus said, "...apart from Me you can do nothing." This teaching reminds us of the last phrase He stated in the Great Commission, "...I am with you always, even to the end of the age" (Mt. 28:20, NASB). Jesus wants us to bear fruit, and He makes it possible for us to bear fruit by empowering us to bear it. The Holy Spirit gives us fruit in our personal lives and then the power to share that fruit with others. Then we see transformation in others, another form of fruit in the harvest. Wholehearted church planters who know and follow Jesus become fruit-bearers because of that knowledge.

Knowing Christ also means knowing His central message about the Kingdom of God. Many people are writing books and doing research on the new generations who are turning away from the Church. I would argue new generations turn away from the Church for one simple reason. They do not turn away because they don't love God. They turn away because what they see lived out in our churches stands in sharp contrast to what they imagine Jesus would emphasize. Not knowing what else to do, they are walking away because we tend to focus on "success" more than on the fruit of abiding in Christ and living for Him daily.

Denominationalism has focused more on drawing lines between people than on the unifying message Jesus gave when He discussed the Kingdom of God. Sometimes pastors and planters get territorial about their churches. This territorialism contrasts with the reality of the Kingdom of God Jesus taught. Church and denominational politics and church disunity contrast to what people innately understand when they see or hear the teaching of the Kingdom of God in the Bible. The new generations of followers of Jesus long to serve Christ in a way that is fresh, unifying, and biblical. Wholehearted church planters are focused on the Kingdom, abiding in Christ, and knowing and following Jesus.

Wholehearted "Followship" and Discipleship in the Church

Being wholehearted in the realm of discipleship means a new church's biblical values are rooted in Jesus' words and ways. In the early 2000s, I was teaching in Phoenix, Arizona. I like to eat international cuisine with my students whenever possible for two reasons. I like the fellowship and friendships that develop, and I like to expose students to food of other cultures. I actually have two personal "rules" for eating food purchased in restaurants: avoid American cuisine (because my wife cooks it so well) and avoid chain restaurants. On this day a small group of students and I went to Tempe, Arizona, across the street from the state university, to eat lunch at a restaurant that advertised Israeli cuisine.

Our server was a young blond man who said his name was Derek. He had a strong accent so I asked him if he was from Israel, following the heritage advertised. He said he was Polish (I clearly didn't know a Polish accent speaking English). I remembered that many Jewish people live in

Poland, so I asked him if he were Jewish. He replied, "No, I am a follower of Jesus."

This unexpected surprise led to an ongoing conversation as Derek came and went from our table throughout the meal. This conversation changed my life and my thinking about being a disciple of Jesus.

I asked Derek if he was a student at the university across the street.

He replied, "No, some friends and I are new followers of Jesus, and we have decided to spend the next two years studying the Bible together."

I asked him what they were studying currently.

He answered, "Well, in the book of John, Jesus said if we love Him, to keep His commandments.[6] We know we love Jesus and want to obey His commands, but we didn't know what they were." He went on to explain, "Someone told us that if we get a Bible with red letters in it, that the red letters are the words of Jesus, so we decided to all get Bibles with red letters and when we came to the red letters to see if the passage held a command of Jesus.. When we find one, we ask ourselves whether we are obeying this command."

This conversation captivated my mind and heart. The rest of the day I could not stop thinking about this encounter. On my flight home later that day I decided I would go home, study the Bible that way, and see what God would teach me. Over the next few months my idea of following Jesus was transformed. A command of Jesus from the red letters confronted me daily. Constantly, Jesus challenged me to see that so much of the Christian culture that I lived and reproduced was on peripheral issues of following Christ. The bulk of Jesus' commands were not central to the common culture of "being Christian." Some of the things I focused upon, while perhaps admirable, were extrabiblical. Some of Jesus' central commands my traditions largely ignored.

This red letter experience was humbling and required a transformation of how I lived and what I taught my church, students, and mentees. I realized that much of what I had done was to train people to be good church members, rather than to be wholehearted followers of Jesus. The questions I most often hold myself accountable to are, "What are the commands of the 'red letters'? Am I living those obediently?"

The rest of the authoritative instructions of Scripture are consistent with those commands and never contradict them. Jesus' commands and example become foundational for making disciples, a basic commandment that Jesus gave as His last words before ascending, and giving us direction until He returns. Wholehearted church planters know Jesus intimately, obediently follow His commands, and along the way teach others to do the same.

Chapter 4

Knowing God's Spirit

ALLAN KARR

Imagination is more important than knowledge... –ALBERT EINSTEIN

Dependency on the Holy Spirit

Years ago during a daily prayer time, Jim Misloski, my prayer partner, introduced me to a truth in Scripture that had been overlooked during my many other previous readings of the passage. We were looking at Luke 11. While teaching His disciples to pray, Jesus made an analogy about a man having an unexpected visitor and begging his neighbor for bread to meet the need of the day. Luke 11:13 jumped off the page in importance that day. "How much more will your Father in Heaven give the *Holy Spirit* to those who ask him!" (emphasis added). This passage was about prayer, but also about the Holy Spirit. We exegeted that scripture for many weeks, discerning what God wanted us to learn. We learned to pray consistently as Jesus taught, but we also learned that the prayer included asking God for empowerment of the Holy Spirit.

"Three Loaves of Bread"

A regular part of my almost daily prayer with Jim is, "God, please give us three loaves of bread." We know that the Holy Spirit transformed us at the moment of new spiritual birth. We know that the Holy Spirit is available to us every moment of every day. We know we could live in that reality. Yet we know these were Jesus' words as He taught His disciples to pray. He taught us to ask God for the Holy Spirit likened unto a person asking a neighbor for three loaves of bread. Scripture offers no detail here, but, in my imagination, the needy man asks God for one "loaf" of the Holy Spirit's power for the day for himself, one "loaf" for his family, and one "loaf" for the other relationships God will bring into his life that day. Why would Jesus teach us to persistently ask for the Holy Spirit, if it were not in the heart of God to answer that prayer?

While praying with Jim recently, he prayed a twist on this prayer that is quite rich. He prayed, "God give us fresh bread to give people today, bread that smells good and is appetizing to those we share it with." What a beautiful image! If we only have stale or moldy bread to share with others, it would not be an attractive representation of the Kingdom. I know that in this analogy, God would never give us old bread as an expression of His Spirit, but we could let it get stale by not getting fresh bread each day. I have started each day now by asking God for fresh, aromatic, appetizing bread for my own day's needs and to have something attractive with which to share the Kingdom with all the people in my divine appointments for the day.

In April 2012, I traveled to India to dig a well and train church planters in this platform. When we were praying for this trip, we realized that we were praying for bread and water, a pretty image of biblical Kingdom truths. We were praying for actual water and "living water," like in John 4:10 when Jesus was talking to the woman at the well. Praying for actual water and living water has become my mainstay prayer daily. This type of prayer reflects how I am learning to walk daily in the power of the Holy Spirit, made possible by who we have become and are in union with Christ.

Fear of Abuse of the "Spirit"

Many evangelical Christians and groups fear or greatly disagree with what they see as abuses of the doctrine of the Holy Spirit in faith practices of daily or regular meeting of congregations. Many Christians have overreacted to this fear and now virtually ignore this central truth of who we are now in our union with Christ. We have the power of the Holy Spirit available to us every minute of every day and yet many ignore that reality for fear of being "charismatic" or "Pentecostal," both labels that many Evangelicals see as having a negative connotation. These anti-charismatic believers try to distance themselves from a practice of doctrine that they see as being either problematical or in error or both. In so doing many sincere people have distanced themselves from living in the reality and the blessing of being dependent and empowered by the Holy Spirit in their daily lives.

My microcommunity believes that the Holy Spirit is alive and well, operating every minute of every day in this world as part of the Kingdom of God. If this is not true, then why do we pray at all? Why do we pray to God for those in our lives who are sick or injured, if God can't answer those prayers? I serve, worship, and give testimony to a living, powerful God who still does miracles on a regular basis as standard operating procedure. If this isn't true, we are spending an enormous amount of energy on a wasted cause. My God, including the person of the Holy Spirit, is powerful and active in the lives of those whom He has transformed.

Imagining What Is Already True

One day I was teaching a class of church planters. I had invited my mentor Kenny Moore to help present this material of the presence of the Holy Spirit. We asked the class to imagine what was already true: that all three parts of the Trinity– Father, Son and Holy Spirit–were present and active in the lives of those in God's family, that is, they were somehow present in that room as well as with each person as they went about their lives. We then asked the students to imagine what difference it would make in our lives, in our ministry, in the lives of those we work with, if we really believed that when we were born again that we were resurrected–right now–just as Jesus was. We also asked them to imagine that, if we truly were resurrected at conversion, then we are now in the company/community of the Trinity. We asked, "What difference would that reality make in our lives, in our ministry, and in the lives of those we work with?" I stood at the whiteboard with marker in hand waiting to write down the class's answers. The class was silent for a few moments while people processed their answers. Finally, someone spoke up. Gradually the dialogue started to gain momentum, and the whiteboard began to fill up. At the end of a lively and inspiring session of dialogue, the whiteboard was full. The Holy Spirit had engaged the imagination of the students. They had described a life that looked exciting, yet truly a biblical picture of the life God intends His family to live. Their responses included,

"Since that is true, we would pray more in regular interaction with God who is with us always."

"We would pray with more faith and boldness."

"We would be more courageous and bold in sharing our faith."

"We would be fearless and have more courage to be obedient to the direction God gives our lives."

"We would be more generous."

"We would be more aware of injustice and more active in addressing those needs."

"More lives would be changed."

"Communities would be healthier."

The answers indicated the class's new imagination. The class had begun to picture a life in union with Christ, in fellowship with the Father, and empowered by the Holy Spirit. They had grown in their thinking. Could they grow in their obedience? Could they live out their imagination? All the answers reflected all the qualities of "greatheartedness."

The Presence of the Holy Spirit of the Trinity

You can exercise the imagination of what is already true in the context of being in the presence of the Holy Spirit who resides with us. Most Christians would cognitively agree that as Christians God is with us. We would likely acknowledge that God is with each of us where we are. We would agree that inexplicably He is with us where we are and that simultaneously He is with our friends on the other side of the globe.

We affirm God's omnipresence. This truth is something only understood or believed by faith. While we say we believe it, we often forget it is true. Another prayer lies in God's heart ready for Him to answer. In this prayer we ask the Holy Spirit to remind us of what is already true of us–that we are in the presence of the Holy Spirit.

In an effort to remember this truth daily, I started to use my imagination. I ride in my car everyday to commute to work and to carry out everyday errands. My car comfortably seats four people. To remember that I am in the presence of the Trinity, I imagine that the Father, Son, and Holy Spirit are occupying the other three seats in the car as I drive down the road.

This exercise in imagination changes my perception of reality. It changes the way I pray. Prayer becomes an intimate conversation (casual in tone, as opposed to formal) as I ride down the road, much like it would be if I had a human passenger. Prayer becomes conversational between the Trinity and myself. I ask for advice and then listen for the answer. This exercise of my imagination helps me to realize what is already true. We live in the presence of the Holy Spirit. Sometimes I even chuckle as I try to imagine which person of the Trinity is riding "shotgun." Can you imagine us walking out to the car and having Jesus exclaim, "Shotgun!" as He hurries to the passenger front seat? I get to drive because I have skin on, but the Trinity is with me wherever I go all day long.

Living cognizant of the presence of the Trinity changes the way we live in many ways. I am more aware of my words, whether they are edifying or not. The practice of the presence of the Trinity holds me accountable to live with integrity knowing that the Father, Son, and Holy Spirit are walking around with me, even looking over my shoulder. I am more responsive when a gentle suggestion of the Spirit prompts me to be generous or kind in helping someone in word and deed. I am bolder as a witness of the truth of the gospel when I am directed to be intentional. Living empowered by the Holy Spirit and aware of His presence is part of what it means to be wholehearted.

The Power of the Holy Spirit

I always thought of the book of Acts as simply a history of the Church and works of the apostles until I read Roland Allen's *The Ministry of the Spirit*.[1] I was surprised to recognize Allen's point that Acts is actually focused on the Holy Spirit as the missionary agent. These words made his point stick:

> Our conception of the work of the Holy Spirit has been almost confined to the revelation of truth, of holiness, of church government and order. Missionary work as an expression of the Holy Spirit has received such slight and casual attention that it might

> almost escape the notice of a hasty reader... For it is in the revela-
> tion of the Holy Spirit as a missionary Spirit that the Acts stands
> alone in the New Testament... In the Acts it is the one prominent
> feature... To treat it as secondary destroys the whole character and
> purpose of the book.[2]

The Holy Spirit is mentioned all through the Bible, from Genesis to Rev-
elation. The Spirit is not just a post-Pentecost dispensational tool of God
that is no longer active. The Spirit of God was present and active in creation and vital to understanding God in the ancient period, in every period since, *as well as* in the postmodern era in which we live.

Many of the founding fathers of the United States identified themselves
as "Deists." They believed in a Creator, but their worldview assumed that
this higher power was no longer active in the everyday environment in
which we live. The analogy of a "clockmaker" is commonly used.

> Deists believe in a god of nature—a noninterventionist creator—
> who permits the universe to run itself according to natural laws.
> Like a "clockmaker god" initiating the cosmic process, the uni-
> verse moves forward, without needing God's supervision.[3]

The idea is that the Creator made the world, started it in motion, and
stands back to watch it work, much like a clockmaker who made a clock,
set it in motion, and then watches it keep time.

Some people argue that we are now in a dispensation where the Holy
Spirit is no longer active and powerful. In this view the Spirit is only something God used for a season in the book of Acts to get the Church started.
That belief implies that miracles no longer occur, God no longer answers
prayers, or worse that He hears them and is powerless to answer them.
Very little separates a deist from those who espouse this dispensational
theology. In both cases, God is no longer active, no longer performing
miracles, no longer hearing our prayers and answering them. I categori-
cally refuse to embrace these powerless ideas of theology. They are not
consistent with our understanding of Scripture or wholeheartedness.

Functional Deism

Most Evangelicals would argue that they are neither Deists nor "dispen-
sationalists." If you asked them if they believed in prayer, they would
say, "Yes!" If you asked them if God was powerful, they would agree.
However, if you were able to monitor and measure their prayers, many
Christians shockingly pray very infrequently. Their faith to believe God
answers prayers is startlingly weak. They stand surprised, even mystified
when they see evidence that God does answer a prayer. If we live outside
of the realization of the presence of the Holy Spirit or without a dependence on the power of the Holy Spirit, we actually practice a form of

"functional deism." While on the one hand we cognitively believe God is powerful and hears and answers our prayers, in daily reality we function as deists. Our lives witness only to a God who created the world but is no longer active in it.

"Wholeheartedness" acknowledges the reality of the Holy Spirit who transformed us, is present with us, empowers us, and even still performs miraculous acts, acts which can be attributable only to the power of the God of the universe. I believe in the Holy Spirit who is active and powerful, and it is consistent with my experiences of the Spirit and with what the Bible teaches. This is the God I know and why I worship. This God empowers us to be greathearted. Wholehearted church planters understand that we serve and proclaim a mighty God, and we are not Him. They know that their ministry is directed and empowered by the Holy Spirit.

Spiritual Warfare

A large part of being wholehearted as a church planter is being active in prayer focused on "spiritual warfare." This is a big part of the wholehearted church planter's work. A couple of weeks after we moved to Castle Rock, Colorado, to plant a church, I met a Christian woman who was a friend but not part of our new church. She told me that my church planting family was an answer to her prayers. She told me that she had been praying for many years that God would bring a new church to Castle Rock. She was praying against spiritual forces that wanted to prevent an expansion of God's Kingdom in her city. We realized then that our family being called to Castle Rock was even a bigger divine design than we had previously understood. God was planning a new church in Castle Rock, and He asked my family to be a part of the plan. However, I now realized that if I had been disobedient, and *not* responded to God's call, that God would have still planted a church in Castle Rock. God's plan was not dependent upon me or my family; however, He wanted to bless us to be a part of His answer to many prayers prayed before we even considered church planting.

Another event made me realize the significance of spiritual warfare in wholehearted church planting. I became part of a pastor's fellowship in our city made up of Evangelical pastors with similar doctrines. As a group, we valued prayer and wanted to connect relationally in leading our churches to pray for our county to have a Christian-based spiritual awakening. We decided to prayerwalk the county lines, to do spiritual warfare symbolically and in reality, surrounding our county in prayer. This required that each church in the fellowship be responsible for covering approximately twenty miles of the county line in prayerwalking. Many of the county lines were literally roads that were relatively easy to prayerwalk. The western side of our county was all in very mountainous terrain with limited access by road. I volunteered our church to cover twenty miles of the most difficult section of the county lines to prayerwalk. We divided up the twenty miles into several sections and then went on the agreed-upon day to our areas to walk and pray as the Holy Spirit directed, but focusing on spiritual warfare for our county. What I learned that day was very significant. Our "new" work reflected a long history of spiritual barriers that went back many generations in my community.

Colorado has an interesting history, as do most communities and regions. To begin with, we can point back to a long history of Native American spiritualism, much of which focused on animistic religions of the first nation peoples. While prayerwalking, I twice encountered totem poles in spiritual sacred spots of Native American religions. Evangelicals have generally done a terrible job of sharing the gospel in a culturally appropriate contextual way with Native Americans. I am totally aware that the religion of the indigenous people includes a higher Being, but I know full well that their view of "god" is not consistent with Scripture on the crucial issues of salvation. To prepare the soil of people's hearts for the seed of the gospel, my county needed prayers of spiritual warfare against centuries-old strongholds. Additionally, when non-natives started to invade this territory, they usually came for very selfish reasons. The Spanish and White Americans came with greedy motives looking for quick riches in gold and other precious minerals. They came to rob the wealth of the wildlife, such as the American bison. They trapped and exploited and endangered other animals such as beaver and other fur-bearing game. They came to claim the land as their own, when for millennia an indigenous culture had shared the land and lived in harmony with it. In our prayerwalking, we encountered mines and trapper cabins. The Holy Spirit taught us that much of the new culture that had invaded the native culture was from the sinful nature of man: greed and exploitation. Even the contemporary resorts in our state have some of the same motives. We realized our prayer needed to include a generational confession and apology in asking for forgiveness of the bad motives and actions of our previous generations. Perhaps a spiritual awakening in our county will not happen until some of these past issues are confronted and cleansed. Similar issues plague your community, whether urban or rural, and form part of your wholehearted spiritual responsibility.

Finally, Colorado has for over a century become a place of security and retreat for many groups on the periphery of society that face severe spiritual challenges. While prayerwalking we found a "church" for white supremacist Satan worshipers. It was in a very remote area, but wasn't trying to be hidden—as displayed by the signage they put up. Our county has many similar spiritually unhealthy groups of people. In our county, we are now about 40 percent Mormon, who proclaim themselves "Christian." Yet while saying they are the *Church of Jesus Christ of Latter Day Saints*, they have a fundamentally nonbiblical doctrine of the gospel and of salvation.

We have New Age philosophies, uniquely American versions of Buddhism, and various forms of non-Christian spiritual ideologies. We realized that the coming of a Christian awakening in our county required us to pray against the false religions that are quite present and that proclaim their versions of truth that are distinctively not following the truths of Scripture or the teachings of Jesus. As a church planter, your context will be different from Colorado, yet there will inevitably be a spiritual reality in your historical context that needs a wholehearted commitment to spiritual warfare. This is an important part of living in the reality of the power of the Holy Spirit.

The Holy Spirit's Vision and Strategy

The vision for any new church comes from God's heart and is implanted in the hearts of the whole church planting team by the power of the Holy Spirit. Sometimes people talk about God's will as if it is a mysterious secret that is hard to discover. However, we suggest that God wants to reveal His will and that, as we walk daily in the power of the Spirit, the divine will is not so mysterious. The Spirit can even work through our partners. We suggest that some of the ways the Spirit works in the lives of individuals is done through the roles good partner/sponsor churches can play in the lives of the churches they start. Through our partners, the Holy Spirit can guide, teach, empower, comfort, and intercede in the lives of wholehearted church planters. God's vision is given to us as we live in the reality of the Holy Spirit. The strategy for any new church also comes from God's heart and is implanted in the hearts of the whole church planting team. Second Peter 1:21 says, "For prophecy never had its origin in the human will, but prophets, though human, spoke from God as they were carried along by the Holy Spirit."

Perhaps it seems superfluous to focus so much on the Holy Spirit, especially when there is an ever-present danger of being misunderstood because the Evangelical culture has often shied away from focusing on the Holy Spirit because of unbiblical or abusive practices historically in the Church. However, there may be no more important chapter in this book. Church planters are only wholehearted by the power of the Holy Spirit. We are not transformed by our own power, we cannot receive salvation through our own power, and we cannot change our community or the lives of other people without the power of the Holy Spirit. This is who we are in Christ. Wholehearted church planters realize this and live in that reality.

Chapter 5

The Response of Worship and Work

ALLAN KARR

Human knowledge must be understood to be loved, but divine knowledge must be loved to be understood. –PASCAL

The Luke 10:27 Call

Jesus was a masterful teacher! He used a variety of techniques to make disciples. The tenth chapter of Luke is full of treasures for the church planter. Corey Best, a former student of mine, is a great missionary church planter in Switzerland. Years after leaving my class, he told me an amusing, yet convicting fact that has happened ever since he took my classes. When he lays his Bible down, it automatically falls open to Luke 10. Corey's experience has so many truths for disciples of Jesus, especially for those wanting to sharpen their missionary skills.

In the latter half of Luke 10, Jesus is in a teaching dialogue with those around him. He often answers questions with questions. In answering one of Jesus' questions, a "lawyer" quoted passages of the Old Testament; Luke 10:27 says:

> You shall love the LORD your God with all your heart, and with all your soul, and with all your strength, and with all your mind; and your neighbor as yourself. (NASB)[1]

We refer to this passage as the "Luke 10:27 Call." This passage is rich with all its implications of how to live as a follower of Jesus. Understanding the content of the Luke 10:27 Call is foundational as a response to knowing God. Wholehearted church planters respond to God in a way that builds on this foundational passage.

Worship as a Wholehearted Response to the Person of God

Ask most church planters to tell you about their church, and you get common answers. The church planter usually starts to describe the gathering, the place, or the programs. Specific attention will be given the "worship" service. Too often "worship" is limited to the one dimensionality of the relatively short amount of time each week that a church gathers together and has some elements of music, singing, liturgy, prayer, scripture reading, and preaching. A church planter often takes care to mention "creative" elements of their worship–drama, technology, videos, and lighting. To some, worship services have become showy performances that represent the entirety of their understanding of worship. The wholehearted church planter sees in such answers a shallow understanding of this beautifully holistic expression of knowing God. Worship is not simply a program of the church. Simultaneously, worship includes both a *simple* response by believers who are in Christ and at the same time a *complex* response that resonates at every level of who we holistically are as people in the Kingdom.

Sometimes people want to use Matthew 18:20 to define either "church" or "worship." Jesus said, "For where two or three have gathered together in My name, I am there in their midst" (NASB). Using this definition for either "church" or "worship" is shallow and incomplete. For several years I have defined church in words similar to these: *The church is a microcommunity of transformed followers of Jesus, who perceive themselves to be the body of Christ in their macrocommunity and in the global context, and live as such.* The church is not just the church when it is gathered; it is the church all week long in every context of life.

When I was a child, I learned a children's ditty about the church, complete with hand motions of fingers intertwined, along with steepled index fingers. The ditty says:

> *This is the church* (showing the hands intertwined in the "shape" of a church building).
> *This is the steeple* (wiggling steepled index fingers).
> *Open the doors* (hinging the thumbs open),
> *And see all the people* (turning interconnected hands over and wiggling the intertwined fingers).

The problem with the ditty is that it is at best "wrong" and at worst heretical in what it teaches to children. I changed the ditty as I taught it to my own children when they were small. Now when I teach my new version of this poem to other children, I use the exact same hand motions and say these words:

> This is the building.
> This is the steeple.
> Open the doors.
> *The Church is God's people.*

I then undo my intertwined fingers, spread my hands apart while still wiggling my fingers, and say, "And we are the church all week long when we go to our homes, and neighborhoods, and schools, and workplaces." The church is not the church *only* when it is gathered. By the sheer amount of time alone, the church is actually more the church when it is not gathered.

Similarly, if we limit the idea of worship to just the regular congregational gathering, we are forgetting the entire rest of the week. A week embraces 168 hours, and we gather as a church at best only three to five hours of that. Many people have the idea that worship is something happening only in a church service. Many people only define worship as the part of the worship service that involves music and singing. In truth, worship in much more than that. Worship is a lifestyle, a wholehearted response of a person answering the Luke 10:27 Call, and in a loving relationship with the Persons of God.

Occasionally, when I am teaching this principle, a student will point out that out of the 168 hours in a week, many of them are spent sleeping, so the principle is flawed. However, it should be pointed out that a person can be sleeping in the wrong bed with the wrong person, and not be honoring God in his or her life. If worship is seen as a holistic response to the Persons of God, then it is a 24/7 lifestyle. Worship is not an event of the week. Worship is a lifestyle enhanced by a corporate gathering that adds focus and energy to the rest of the week's worship activities.

God's People Are Worshipers

The wholehearted person of God and follower of Jesus cannot help but love, worship, obey, and serve Him. Worship is part of what happens to us when God reaches down from heaven and opens our hearts to believe. It is a part of the transformation that occurs in us when we are born afresh in our spirit by the power of the Holy Spirit. Being a worshiper is part of the definition of what it means to be the people of God. Worship is not a subset or an occasional activity of being a wholehearted follower of Christ. Worship should be seen as synonymous to whom we already are in Christ.

I (Allan) pray regularly with several people. We are aware that, as we worship God in this intimate communication with Him, we come to know God more and more. Worship gains momentum. Like a snowball rolling downhill, worship gets bigger and bigger, gaining speed and power as it does. The more you know God, the more wholehearted you become, the more you worship, and the stronger the cyclical momentum increases. For wholehearted people, this kind of dynamic worship deepens one's faith. Wholehearted church planters understand this and model and teach this concept of worship to the people in their churches.

A popular staff position in churches, often of vocational ministry, is a Worship Pastor, often called the Minister of Music. Dozens of creative names are tied to this position. The vast majority of people perceive that this title means that the person in this position is responsible only to plan and organize the music portions of a church service. This perception is strengthened because many people commonly limit the word *worship* to the context of music in the church service. This is such an anemic understanding of a rich and dynamic biblical truth. Worship is not just music; it is a lifestyle.

Wholehearted church planters structure their churches to realize that worship is not just a few minutes in a church service, or even limited to the gathering of believers. The vast majority or worship takes place when the church members leave the gathering and live their lives the rest of the week in their homes around their families, in their workplaces around their coworkers, in their schools around their peers, and in their communities with their neighbors. The rest of the world who are not followers of Jesus need to see that the people of God worship in every context of their lives They need to understand and experience that our worship is comprehensive, not just limited to singing a hymn or a praise song. Worship is a constant posture of being holistically honoring to God, giving praise to Him rather than taking credit in a selfish way. Wholehearted church planters understand how vital worship is to the life of the church plant. A church planter must live this daily and incorporate this value into the life of the body of Christ. Worship is a response of wholeheartedness. Being wholehearted results in being a worshiper. Such experience of worship creates a powerful cycle in the Kingdom of God.

A Wholehearted Work Ethic

My father's generation valued a strong work ethic almost to the point of veneration. Growing up as a male in the last half of the twentieth century, I was taught that working hard was expected of everyone, and even became a point of pride for a young man. In 1997, I was working very hard and was having some "success" as a church planter. However, when I compared our church plant to others that were glorified nationally, I felt a private sense of failure. My flesh response to this was to work harder. By the fall of that year, I was experiencing burnout. I sought the counsel of my mentors[2] and, upon reflection, discovered that my work ethic was a flesh response, although it looked positive to most people.

If we try to carry a burden that only God can bear, it is a flesh response. We cannot do God's job because we are not He. If we try by working harder, we will be burned out quickly, and the job will not be done. In Matthew 21:21, Jesus was teaching on prayer and said that God could take a mountain and throw it into the sea. If we tried to throw the mountain into the sea by ourselves, we would fail. If we decided to work harder, we would still fail and would quickly be exhausted. The church is full of leaders who have tried to carry God's burdens by working harder. The fruit of the Holy Spirit is contrasted in Scripture with the deeds of the flesh. Galatians 5 is a primary text for these teachings. We usually have the idea that "flesh" all looks negative, like adultery or greed. However, some "flesh" strategies of coping with life and ministry look positive. There is nothing wrong with education, unless you trust in the degrees for success more than in who we are in Christ. There is nothing wrong with being a great communicator, unless you rely on that strength instead of trusting in God to make disciples. Some "flesh" responses look positive.

Working hard is a common flesh response that looks positive to the world. As a pastor, even in times when my life was out of balance and in danger of damaging family relationships, my congregations were patting me on the back with compliments about how hard I was working. Coupled with my cultural upbringing, working harder was a recipe for walking in the "positive-looking" flesh and burning out. Wholeheartedness understands how to have a strong work ethic that is holistically healthy and empowered by God's Spirit. A new lesson with that understanding has to be refreshed almost daily, as the temptation to respond to the stress of life is to work harder rather than trust in God. Nothing is wrong with working hard unless it becomes that upon which we put our faith instead of who we are in Christ. "Work ethic" is an issue that needs balance.

In a later chapter, the issue of being a workaholic is further addressed as a wholehearted issue in the context of the family, but many church planters struggle with finding a healthy way to address this issue. There is nothing wrong with working hard and being tired at the end of a day. God made us to enjoy working hard. But whenever I start feeling burned out even a little, I use it as a red flag to examine my life to see if I am lapsing into a flesh response that is not wholehearted.

The Other Side of the Coin

The "work ethic" coin has another side. Many church planters and missionaries struggle with having a weak work ethic. The Psalms and Proverbs are full of wisdom extolling the dangers of being lazy or slothful. We are not suggesting that to avoid getting burned out you should just be passive and sit around waiting for God to move the mountain. A biblical and wholehearted response to knowing God is to listen to what God instructs, and then to obey quickly and work passionately in His will and empowerment. Having a strong work ethic is another response of the wholehearted person of God. However, the other end of the spectrum is the issue of having a strong work ethic that honors the principles of the Luke 10:27 Call. Working hard and seeing fruit we know came from God is a sweet blessing from God. Enjoying our work is a response of the planter who knows and loves God.

I teach seminary students at five campuses in the United States and on about a dozen campuses internationally. Generally speaking, I teach students who are devoted to God and brimming with talent and potential. The demographics at each campus are unique. Several of the schools have student bodies containing students predominantly in their twenties, with a good percentage of them single. Inevitably in the Christian context, single women strongly outnumber single men. I occasionally ask the single women why they are so dominant on campus. Their answers echo a repeating theme that at first surprised me.

One Christian young lady said, "My theory is video games!" Puzzled, I asked her to explain. She said a vast majority of young women are serious about God, serious about their service in ministry, serious about their studies, and are working to fulfill their passions in a way that honors God. She further explained that many of those women have observed that single men of their same age spend a majority of their time and energy hanging out playing video games with their roommates and friends, even in the seminary dorms.

I have heard this same critique with a similar theme from young women all over the world. While an older generation struggled to balance their work ethic in a way that wasn't overbalanced into "workaholism," the younger generation is struggling to have a work ethic that honors God wholeheartedly. While video games cannot necessarily be blamed for a lifestyle that doesn't honor God, they are a symptom and a contributing cause of a generation of young people struggling with their work ethic. We are seeing a younger generation who needs to be intentional to ensure their response to God in the context of their work ethic is wholehearted.

The work style of the wholehearted church planter is courageous, committed, competent, and constant. A large part of the wholehearted work ethic is to be intrinsically motivated. People who are intrinsically motivated are persistent when they meet challenges, and resilient when disappointments arise. Intrinsic motivation means the planter is willing to exert high energy and effort when the season calls for it. The planter desires to do well and is even willing to be aggressive, without the negative aspects of task orientation.

Many church planters have moved into a new community to plant a new church. The strategy of the planter is to develop relationships and organize the new church. The neighbors in the surrounding community may think the planter just sits at home or goes to drink coffee with friends. Getting involved with a community and being diligent in the tasks God directs help the community see the planter as a valuable and caring part of the local society. God often uses this platform of social involvement to plant the new church. The wholehearted church planter works diligently, not out of personal drive or ambition (flesh), but out of love and obedience to God empowered by the Holy Spirit. Wholehearted church planters long for the Father's commendation, "Well done, good and faithful servant." This commendation comes when the work ethic is balanced, biblical, and healthy.

Every Christ Follower an Incarnational Missionary[3]

In a later chapter on knowing yourself, my co-author will expound on the idea that being wholehearted is not just for church planters. Being wholehearted is for all followers of Jesus. In a similar train of thought, being a church planting missionary is not just for some people. The Great Commission of Jesus is not just for those who are called to be missionaries, or church planters, or are gifted in evangelism. The command is for every Christ follower. The wholehearted response is that all followers of Jesus are called to love God, all called to love their neighbors, all called to love themselves, and all called to get involved in their communities. All Christ followers are called to be salt and light, and messengers of the gospel. This is what it means to be an incarnational missionary, and to fulfill the Luke 10:27 Call.

Conclusion

Wholeheartedness is a cyclical process of knowing God and responding to God in ways that result in knowing God more. The Luke 10:27 Call to the follower of Christ designs a lifestyle where the wholehearted response is a life of holistic worship and a balanced work ethic that is empowered by the Spirit. This diligent lifestyle is dedicated to obeying God passionately. Wholehearted church planters know these truths, but we can still be held accountable to be (become) who we already are in Christ by being reminded of these biblical principles. We hope that this chapter is a reminder to our readers to live in these truths.

Chapter 6

Knowing a People and Their Place

LINDA BERGQUIST

...before we plow an unfamiliar patch,
It is well to be informed about the winds,
About the variations in the sky,
The native traits and habits of the place,
What each locale permits, and what denies.[1]

In his graphic novel series, *The Sandman*, Neil Gaiman offers this observation:

> I've been making a list of the things they don't teach you at school. They don't teach you how to love somebody... They don't teach you how to know what's going on in someone else's mind. They don't teach you what to say to someone who's dying. They don't teach you anything worth knowing."[2]

We have so much to learn about church planting that "they don't teach you at school"– not in church planting boot camps, practicum, or at seminary. While these venues offer a lot that is worth studying, they generally focus on only a few ways for future church planters to learn about people and places. Culture exegesis is a skill that helps church planters know the people who form any community. The word *exegesis* literally means "to draw out." We move inside of a culture to draw out information about it. The best way to practice exegesis is asking good questions and listening to stories. This process covers topics such as worldviews, values, allegiances, ethics, aesthetics, how decisions are (and should be) made, cultural practices and behaviors, icons, perceptions of the gospel, and other aspects of a culture that affect church planting strategies.[3]

In this chapter Linda and Allan aim to present a multifaceted perspective regarding cultural exegesis. We offer objective (quantitative), subjective (qualitative), and spiritual ways of knowing a community deeply, empathetically, and hopefully. By objective information, we echo the words made famous by the character Joe Friday in the 1950s television show *Dragnet,* "Just the facts, Ma'am." Objective, concrete information is worth a lot, and good interpretation of information–or reason and logic– is worth even more. Here we will share resources that can help church planters and their partner churches gather helpful kinds of information. However, factual data is not everything. Subjective information is also critical. By subjective we mean information that is not as easily measured and is gleaned personally, emotionally, relationally, or intuitively. Finally, church planters come to know their communities spiritually through prayer and listening to God. The Spirit imparts not only wisdom, but also the faith to believe in His voice.

Spiritual Knowledge

The spiritual dimension of planting a church among a people begins long before a church planter enters the picture. God cares about a place before humans are ever involved. He desires that it be known, loved, and transformed by the gospel. Others, such as partnering churches, Christian neighbors, and strategy teams also become part of the story. Hopefully, they have bathed that community with prayer and are ready to see God work. When the eyes of their hearts have been opened, they begin to see their surroundings more like God sees them. The best way to describe how God spiritually informs church planting strategies is through a series of stories about calling, prayerwalking, and obtaining spiritual access to a community.

The Call to a Community

The church planter's divine call to a particular community is most often spiritually discerned. Vancouver, British Colombia, was not even on the radar for Jerry and Diana Conner when they were finishing seminary in Texas. However, as they began searching for a place to start a church, Vancouver kept coming up. Through the prayers of a seminary professor, connections of friends, former members of their church, and an evangelism class, Vancouver kept surfacing as a place where new churches were needed. One thing happened after another. After much prayer and several visits to Vancouver, the Conners were certain God was calling them there. Their exploration narrowed their search further to the Kitsilano neighborhood of the city. Church planting experts advised the Conners that this might be the most formidable of all Canadian neighborhoods for an American to plant a church, so the couple prayed some more. Again they sensed that God was definitely leading them to Kitsilano. The task was difficult, requiring much patience and courage, but today, a church thrives in Kitsilano.

Prayerwalking

One day while Jorvan Smith was driving on a California freeway, he felt impressed to get off at a particular exit and drive through a town called Hawaiian Gardens. As he drove, Jorvan sensed God's call to plant a church in that place. He could tell immediately that he did not fit the demographic profile of this Hispanic/Filipino/other Asian community. He confirmed this later through a demographic search, which showed that only 1 percent of Hawaiian Gardens matched Jorvan's own African American roots. Yet, as he prayed about it, he became even more convinced that God was calling him to start a church there.

When Jorvan met with church planting strategist Don Overstreet to share his burden for planting a church in Hawaiian Gardens, Don's immediate thought was that Jorvan was not a match for the community. He sent the prospective church planter home to continue praying. When Jorvan returned a few weeks later, even more convinced of God's will, Don said, "We cannot out-argue God, so let's do it."

Jorvan developed a strategy and recruited a team. Don taught the team how to prayer-walk, which they began to do regularly. Jorvan met all kinds of people as he prayed for Hawaiian Gardens—the police chief, the mayor, and other community members who shared their needs with him. He was also able to find a building to rent. Within a few months, an indigenous church was birthed that continues to grow and reach its community.

Spiritual Access to Knowing a Community: Linda's Stories

In 1984, when I (Linda) first began working with Cambodian refugees, the culture was completely foreign to me and to everyone I knew. I gleaned all the information I could, but since I spoke no Cambodian, and only a few people spoke any English, it was difficult to learn all I wanted to know about the group's recent experience, their needs, or their religion. Early on, I met a woman named Chhean (a pseudonym) with whom I shared a kind of spiritual rapport. Chhean and I often visited new refugees together, prayed for them, and brought them rice and vegetables. One day we visited a new family. While I was praying in English, God seemed to be telling me to buy fruit for the new family. I tried to ignore the voice because I had only $5 to my name. Then Chhean prayed in her language. At the close of her prayer, she looked at me and said, "God says, 'Buy fruit.'" I got the idea and immediately obeyed. From then on, Chhean and I always related on a deeply spiritual level. I traveled with her, and she helped me to gain access to the culture.

One day Chhean and I visited a home to pray for an extremely lethargic woman who was supposedly dying. After we prayed, I noticed the medicine on her bedside table. Prescribed for an allergic reaction, the medicine also caused drowsiness. The sleepier the woman became, the sicker her family thought she was, and the more medicine they gave her. I immediately took away the medicine. By the next day she was better. According to that family, my prayers had healed her. Though I meant no such deception, I became a spiritual hero in the community and gained access to its deepest stories.

Subjective Knowledge Through Cultural Immersion

Gathering information is a biblical process. Numbers 13 tells the story of Moses sending out researchers/explorers who represented Israel's twelve tribes. He gave them a specific set of questions that would help them to know about the place where they would eventually live. "See what the land is like and whether the people who live there are strong or weak, few or many. What kind of land do they live in? Is it good or bad? What kind of towns do they live in? Are they unwalled or fortified? How is the soil? Is it fertile or poor? Are there trees in it or not? Do your best to bring back some of the fruit of the land" (Num. 13:18–20).

Moses pushed for the greatest degree of clarification possible. He even asked the team to bring back tangible evidence—fruit that he could taste to evaluate things such as the climate and the acidity of the soil, as well as to evaluate the land's size and condition. This information could only be obtained through a close encounter with the culture, and not from the sidelines.

Today, even though other methods of knowing a place are available, personally seeing with one's own eyes and experiencing with one's other senses are still the best ways of obtaining good information. As this chapter is being written, Jon and Amber, a prospective church planting couple, are driving around a community with Brook, a church planter strategist in training. Together they will look at the homes where people live, an office park where many locals work, and parks where children play. Brook will help Jon and Amber debrief and imagine what it might be like to live in the community.

Although they have already seen the demographic information about the community where they are contemplating planting a church, they can make a valid decision only through personally experiencing the community. They will seek God's will for their lives, and they will consider their time in the community to be a reliable way of gleaning what they need to know to make a valid decision about planting a church there. The couple will surely recognize that the new master-planned community is beautiful, productive, and vitally connected to the larger metropolitan region. Like the researchers who explored Canaan and came back with stories of a land flowing with milk and honey (Num. 13:7), they will certainly be impressed by what they see. They may also find giants there, like an outrageously expensive housing market, powerful executives, and a tough spiritual climate. It may not be the place where God is calling them, but if it is, will they, like Caleb,[4] say, "We should go up and take possession of the land, for we can certainly do it" (Num. 13:30), or will their experience cause them to retreat, as it did most of the other early explorers in the Promised Land?

Continuing in the Cambodian Community

Another story from the early Cambodian refugee community reinforces the point. One day while I was starting the Cambodian church in San Diego, a minor quake shook the earth. I rushed to an apartment complex nearby where many refugees lived and discovered that everyone was inside with their doors locked. Apparently word was out that King Kong was the cause of the shaking earth, and no amount of explanation would change their minds.

Not long after that experience, I entered a room where a beautiful and intelligent Cambodian teen was watching a television show about the universe. For the first time ever, she was encountering the reality that earth was not the only planet, and certainly not the center of the world. "Is it true?" the girl asked. When I assured her that it was, she exclaimed, "I'm so proud of God!" These stories taught me two critical lessons about the community in which I had been commissioned to plant a church. First, I learned the remoteness of the world to which they had been exposed. Second, I learned that for them, at least in 1985, television was an authoritative source. I could only have learned these useful pieces of information by direct cultural immersion in the communities where they lived, and by God's grace. The story of *The Little Prince* offers this piece of advice: "It is only with the heart that one can see rightly; what is essential is invisible to the eye."[5]

Objective Knowledge

The English word *science* comes from the Latin *scientia*, meaning knowledge. Even though the best research is both intuitive and creative, other sources for gathering and utilizing information are also helpful, so this section focuses on the scientific approach. This kind of research helps church planters glean big picture information in fields such as demographics, religious archives, and mapping. Some people, like Linda, enjoy this aspect of learning about a culture, while others are bored or intimidated by it. If you represent the latter, utilize a few fairly pain-free resources that Linda likes to use for gleaning objective information about people and places.

Resources

The U.S. Census Bureau's decadal census is a great source for information.[6] This website first asks for a state name and then takes site users to a link to select a particular county or city. When those results appear, on the top right side of the page, directly above the columns, is "*browse data sets.*" This allows participants to view information about age, education, race, and specific country of origin and then to browse various data sets for more information. The estimates from the American Community Survey given there offer more kinds of data, but they are taken from less complete, less exacting surveys.

A retiring missionary couple wanted to live in a North American city where they could continue to live and work among the people group they had served overseas. Linda pointed them to the Modern Language Association's website,[7] which allows participants to either view a language map or to discover language enrollment in courses at U.S. colleges and universities. The map is somewhat outdated and its estimates are really conservative, but the information is arranged by zip code, so it offers an outstanding color-coded view of concentrations of peoples from thirty-three language groups. It is best utilized to identify large areas of population density for various peoples. This tool can be used to take a first look at a community, and can be combined with other tools for more accurate data.

Diversity Central[8] is a great site with a lot of good information, stories, and resources. Here we suggest using their diversity calendar. Special occasions for various peoples and religions are listed in the calendar. Knowing these can help church planters take advantage of a culture's particular holidays, holy days, and events that provide opportunities for evangelistic encounters, specific prayer, relational interface, and appropriate gift giving.

A Google alert[9] can be set for any tag words a user would like to be delivered to his or her inbox. For example, Linda set one for Marathi, San Jose, California, to discover more about the Marathi people from India who live in San Jose. She discovered South Asian matrimonial pages that suggest that the Marathi in the United States intermarry only among one another, not even with the larger population from India, and that they actually have their own library in the Silicon Valley. The more specific the tag words, the smaller number of results will appear, but they are more likely to be helpful. If you are an avid researcher, and set many Google alerts, consider a separate e-mail address for receiving them in your inbox.

Familypedia[10] is just one site that lists common surnames by nationality. You can also do a search for sites that just list common or traditional surnames for a particular country, language, religion, or people group, and then search for those names in *whitepages.com* or another on-line phone directory to discover how many people with that surname live nearby. This site is useful despite the growing number of people who have unlisted phone numbers or no landlines.

The Association of Religious Data Archives[11] is a site dedicated to providing free religious data about congregations and denominations by United States counties, metro areas, and states, as well as nationwide data.

They also provide links to other such resources. In the city of San Francisco, Youth With a Mission's (YWAM) local director, Tim Svoboda, created a map of every sacred space of any kind in every neighborhood in the entire city.[12] Maybe someone in your city has created such a tool, too.

In New York, Chris Clayman and Meredith Lee studied eighty-two people groups residing in their city and presented it in the book *ethNYcity: The Nations, Tongues, and Faiths of Metropolitan New York*.[13] While written about New York, these same people groups live in many urban contexts across North America. Zip Skinny[14] provides one-click information about any state in the United States, including demographics, comparisons with other zip codes, school information, and maps.

Layers of Cultural Exegesis

At the end of this chapter is a chart developed to show that culture is more layered than monolithic. The chart presents only a partial indicator of perspectives from which to consider a society. For example, Linda is a somewhat postmodernist second-generation American with Scandinavian and Hispanic heritage, raised in a suburban context (but choosing the city to live in now), born in the boomer generation, and baptized a Methodist as an infant. What lines up there? Not much. One of the problems of exegeting complex cultures is that such cultures are less predictable than the traditional cultural centers with which we are more familiar. Exegeting such stereotypical cultures is easier. For example, most people have no mental framework for "poor, college educated, tribal female" or "punk, boomer, rural male." Complexity forces those who study people and places to do so more anthropologically (up close and personal) rather than simply sociologically (broad strokes/more folks). Clearly, while Hispanic/Latino is a census designation, it is not a realistic way to think about reaching a group that have diverse countries of origin, degrees of assimilation, standards of living, or political preferences. Church planters who care about people spend time with them, listen to who they are, and get to know them well. They participate in cultural activities and learn as much as they can, while still remaining true to a Jesus way of life.

Layers of Cultural Exegesis

Worldview
Modern Postmodern Christian Metanarrative Diverse Unified

Cultural of origin
Vietnamese Indonesian Hispanic African American Norwegian

Region of origin or influence
Southwest Bay Area American South Urban Rural Suburbs

Religious Background
Catholic Hindi Jewish Buddhist Baptist Animistic Wiccan Muslim

Communication
Verbal (English Spanish Chinese, etc)   Non Verbal (Attitudes, Behaviors, Social Distance)

Stage of Assimilation
1st generation 2nd generation 3rd generation Bi-cultural Acculturated

Subcultures and Lifestyles
Cultural Creative Hip-hop Goth Punks Ravers Preppers

Sexuality
Straight Gay Bisexual Transsexual Transsgender

Generations
Builder Boomer Buster Millennial X... Y... Z

Values
Moral Philosophical Social Political Environmental Cultural Familial

Socio-Economic Stratification
Upper Class Middle Class Working Poor Welfare Poor Blue Collar

Social Organization
Tribe Band Clan Peasant Society Extended Family Nuclear Family

Education
No Formal Schooling Elementary High School College Postgraduate

Chapter 7

Knowing the Near and the Far People

LINDA BERGQUIST

And today I'm going to talk to you about near and far. –GROVER, FROM
SESAME STREET

Robert Frost's familiar poem "Mending Wall" tells the story of two neighbors who had different opinions on the value of a fence that separated their properties. One man felt no need for a dividing wall, but the other was convinced that clear boundaries (good fences) made for good neighbor relationships. That was all he had ever known. Would mending the wall help them become better neighbors, or would it have the reverse effect? Walls can function to protect and preserve, as in landscaping where a retaining wall keeps back the earth and protects from the elements. Cell walls in plants act like skin, keeping out what is foreign. In houses, walls divide space into rooms. Jesus had a mission to tear down the dividing wall that had separated Jews and Gentiles for centuries. "For he himself is our peace, who has made the two groups one and has destroyed the barrier, the dividing wall of hostility" (Eph. 2:14). The *African Bible Commentary* explains, "[T]he church has been made the centre of unity for all humanity. Human differences in race, ethnicity, tribe and religion are dissolved or broken down in Christ."[1]

Soon after I (Linda) became a Christian, I discovered a verse from Ephesians that resonated with what I believed was God's call on my life. Ephesians 2:17 says, "He came and preached peace to you who were far away and peace to those who were near." At first this verse seemed to mean that I would spend part of my life ministering in California and the rest as an overseas missionary. Later, I wondered if it meant that I was called to live in an international city where both near and far people already lived.

I eventually realized that in Ephesians, the terms "near" and "far" were not geographical, but spiritual, designations. Just four verses earlier in Ephesians, Scripture makes this concept clear: "But now in Christ Jesus you who formerly were far off have been brought near by the blood of Christ" (Eph. 2:13, NASB). In this chapter we will discuss both spiritual and geographic nearness and farness. We will also use these terms to describe relational, sociological, and ideological distance.

Knowing Those Who Are Near

Relationally Near

In certain arenas of life, experiencing nearness is a relatively uncomplicated process. Family is supposed to be that way. Some people are easier for us to understand, appreciate, and love than others, so we connect instinctively with them. Sometimes these people are already Christians. When this circle of relationships includes those who are already a part of our worlds, we naturally think in terms of getting to know them better, inviting them to church, sharing a testimony, or giving a Bible. Churches invite new members to join fellowship groups where they will meet people like themselves.

What credit should you and I receive for loving people who are "just like us"? What about people we really do not care to know well, or those we do not want to see become a part of our church fellowships? Some of us would rather *those* people remain outside of our circles and far away.

The protagonist in Thomas Wolfe's classic story "The Far and the Near" is a railroad engineer who traveled past a certain cottage every day for twenty years, waving as he went by. He had never met the women who lived there, but he began to feel like he knew them. When he finally did meet them, their attitudes were disappointing and disillusioning. His dream about the women simply did not hold up in the real world, where getting near sometimes equates with getting hurt.[2] Many people decide never to get close to people for this very reason. It is a brave step to open one's life to others, and the result is sometimes almost too difficult to bear. Jesus chose nearness to humanity in the Incarnation and was murdered. He chose a particularly close relationship to twelve, and they betrayed or deserted Him.

Geographically Near

Christians are familiar with thinking about mission in terms of geographical proximity. The Great Commission (Mt. 28:18–20) emphasizes that witness to Christ's Kingdom message is for the entire world, from the end of the block to the ends of the earth. Sometimes, though, Christians find it easier to practice bold gospel witnessing when they are with anyone *but* their nearest neighbors. Give us a mission trip to Mexico; let us have at those poor migrant workers. We will come back with stories and numbers. Why is it so much easier to share the gospel in places far away from home? Does it help with the hurdle of rejection if we know we may never again see the witness-ee? After all, didn't we show up with a truckload of used clothing and school supplies—why would they reject us? Or perhaps we perceive ourselves as *better* than they are. After all, our basic human needs are already met. Sharing Christ with those whom we perceive to be most like us can be much more difficult for many Christians. One of the real values of campus organizations is that they teach young people the life-long skill of sharing Christ with their peers. Ministering in geographical proximity, both near and far, can bring out both the best and the worst in us all.

A church planting family was looking for a place to live in their new community. Two other families from their team had already moved into a major apartment complex near the school where the new church planned to meet. The new planter had heard somewhere that he should not live in an apartment because of the reputation for high turnover. Linda recommended that the family rent an apartment there, despite the high turnover rate. Living there gave other residents the opportunity to watch the planting team live out their lives together, practice one-anothering, host events, and begin friendships with other residents. Their geographic proximity to one another facilitated the birth of the church, but it also reinforced their friendships. They experienced the truth of Proverbs 27:10, "Do not forsake your friend or a friend of your family, / and do not go to your relative's house when disaster strikes you– / better a neighbor nearby than a relative far away."

Spiritually Near

Spiritually near people refers to those with similar beliefs, for instance, those with the same basic view of scriptural authority, the Trinity, and salvation. For church planters, this includes leaders from other churches in their communities. Church planting newcomers can learn from pastors and other Christian leaders who have been around for a while and have wisdom, knowledge, and relational networks. Over time, it may be that several churches begin working on projects with other like-hearted congregations. Together they can impact communities better than they could have alone. A number of church planters we know have talked about the wonderful partnership and unity among churches in New York City and have expressed how valuable this kind of relationship is to the body of Christ in that city.

It is easy to fall into the trap of church competition: "Our church has more members, baptizes more, has better music, attracts more young families, or has a more biblical theology than that other church does." Entrepreneurial types, like many church planters, are hardwired for competition, but there is a better way. Church planters need to know other Christian leaders in their communities. They will want to pray for their success, to listen to their stories about the neighborhood, and to encourage them. Scripture points the way: "Do nothing out of selfish ambition or vain conceit. Rather, in humility value others above yourselves" (Phil. 2:3; also see Rom. 12:3; Gal. 6:4).

Ideologically Near

One of the best ways to foster relational closeness is to nurture friendships around a common cause. Who around you shares your passion for justice, racial reconciliation, opposing human trafficking, serving the poor, earth stewardship, international adoption, foster parenting, or something else? Such nurturing differs greatly from a whole church adopting a neighborhood project—for instance, occasionally serving a local school. It is relatively easy to rally around doing something nice for an organization, but what about joining an existing group of people who give themselves away for something that matters to God but is not yet aligned with the cause of Christ?

Jonathan and Sarah are starting a church among Nepali Buddhist refugees (real names are not used in this section). They have led their simple church to serve by giving food away once a week on the streets of their city. They even negotiated with First Baptist Church to allow them a place to cook the food. Through this service, they are developing deep relationships with new immigrants from Nepal. Shane, who is passionate about justice in the prison system, leads a ministry for newly released prisoners, some of whom have now become followers of Christ and formed a church. Sisters Tami and Karla are home school moms. Their passion for home school education has led them to start a network with other home school families who are not Christians. Some of the other parents have discovered that the sisters' lives are consistent with their own home school values. This has opened a door for them to discover Jesus and to begin participating in Tami and Karla's new church. Living this transparently among other families has challenged the sisters to live more wholly and well. Can you see that, in these examples, it is more about living with passion and concern for others than it is about fashioning a church "project" to help a neighborhood?

Knowing Those Who Are Far

Spiritually Far

In 2010, the greatest number of refugees to the United States came from Iraq (18,016), Burma (16,693), Bhutan (12,363), and Somalia (4,884). Some of the Iraqis are persecuted Christians, as are some of the Burmese, like the Karin. However, most are Buddhist, Muslim, and Hindu. This century's immigrants to North America are not primarily European. With the exceptions of large numbers of Latinos and Filipinos, many of whom arrive in North America with a Catholic/Christian worldview, the newcomers are spiritually distant from North America's religious roots. The number of mosques in the United States jumped by 74 percent between 2000 and 2010. Buddhist and Hindu temples or Sikh Gurdwaras have been planted in most major cities in the United States and Canada.

It would be incorrect to call adherents of Islam, Hinduism, Buddhism, and Sikhism *unbelievers*, for they have very distinct beliefs and practices. Most adults from these backgrounds have no close friends who are active Christians. Other spiritually far people are self-proclaimed atheists or agnostics, or they are simply apathetic to spiritual matters. A recent survey in the United States claimed that the number of people who say they are unaffiliated with any faith today (16 percent) is double the number who say they were not affiliated with any religion when they were children. This figure of the unaffiliated becomes one out of four among young adults ages 18–29. Jesus is not even on their radar.

Finally, a significant number of people call themselves Christians and may attend church, but they live as if their faith has no impact on their lives.

The Lord says,

> "These people come near to me with their mouth
>   and honor me with their lips,
>   but their hearts are far from me.
> Their worship of me is based on merely human rules they have
>   been taught" (Isa. 29:13).

These people are also spiritually far from God, but He longs for them to draw near.

Culturally Far

In June 2010, an average of 104,000 foreigners entered the United States each day. This included 3,100 who received immigrant visas that permitted them to become naturalized citizens in five years, plus 99,200 tourists and students. In 2010, migrants comprised 21 percent of Canada's population and 13.5 percent of the population of the United States. They are immigrants and refugees, agricultural farm workers and students, asylum seekers and victims of global trafficking–and they are our neighbors, or maybe they are your parents or your spouse, or you. Linda and Allan share a common passion for the peoples of the earth. Neither of us can imagine living in a homogenous world. Allan travels, teaching church planting all over the world. Linda and her husband have always lived together in incredibly diverse urban neighborhoods. Allan has adopted children from another culture, and Linda's daughter was usually the only Caucasian girl in her classes until she entered high school. Between Linda and Allan, we have worked with church planters from several dozen cultural and racial/

ethnic backgrounds. We want our ministries and our lives to reflect our beliefs that Jesus brings the far and the near together.

LINDA'S STORY

A few months after I became a follower of Jesus, I became aware that I was part of God's global mission. I was on the Apache reservation, as I mentioned in chapter 1. One afternoon, the Apache co-pastor of the church walked out from his trailer, his face glowing. "What were you just doing?" I asked. "I was reading the Bible and daydreaming about the time when every knee will bow and everyone will call Jesus Christ their Lord," he said (Phil. 2:10). "Jesus was walking down a street among thousands and thousands of people. As He got nearer, all the people started to kneel. People were there from all over the world. Nobody was left out." When I listened to this story and read that verse, a huge "I want" sprang up in my heart. Nothing has ever overshadowed that desire of seeing every nation, tribe, and language united under the Lordship of Christ.

What if every real Christian in the world simply invited a culturally distant family into his or her home to share a meal just a few times a year. How would it change our relationships and our capacity to minister in the name of Jesus? For two years, a Japanese family lived near Linda and Eric while the husband/father studied at a hospital. They celebrated several holidays with us. The first time they ever visited a church, the three boys and the dad, Tetsuro, played shepherds in a Christmas pageant.

When our family visited Japan a few years later, they graciously hosted us and took us to visit Tetsuro's mother. Within five minutes after we met, this old Japanese woman said to me, "My son says you are associated with Christians." "Yes," I replied, "I am a Christian." She told me that when she had lived in Texas forty years ago, she connected with a Baptist church during her two-year stay. Then she said something really astounding. " I am near the end of my life, and now I realize that while I have a religion, the people in that church had a faith. Will you tell me about your faith?" The members of that Texas church will never realize this side of heaven the impact they had on one Japanese woman. "Do not mistreat or oppress a foreigner, for you were foreigners in Egypt" (Ex. 22:21).

Socioeconomically Far

There are two kinds of socioeconomically far people–the poor and the wealthy. Not only are they far from each other, but we would also venture to guess that they are also far from most people who read this book. Convention holds that most churches are able to attract three contiguous socioeconomic groups from upper-upper to lower-lower class. However, some churches seem to embrace a far wider span. What kinds of churches are best able to unite people across a broad socioeconomic spectrum?

1. *Downtown churches.* This is especially true about dense, walkable neighborhoods where all people can easily walk in, and where anyone can arrive via public transportation.
2. *Ideological inclusion.* Churches in some places discover that one way to reach the rich is to embrace and serve poor people. The church begins with a ministry and invites the affluent to participate and donate.
3. *Participatory churches.* When churches involve congregants in broader learning styles than reading and teaching, more kinds of people find the church accessible. Catholic churches pass the peace, genuflect, and engage in repetitious or liturgical practices that widen the church doors. More charismatic style churches engage in practices that involve the use of their bodies and not just their minds–dancing, raising hands, being slain in the Spirit, for example.
4. *Churches that really believe that Jesus values all people.* These churches understand His Kingdom message, "The Spirit of the Lord is on me, because he has anointed me to proclaim good news to the poor" (Lk. 4:18). They emphasize not just reaching the poor, but helping and advocating for them. The Bible contains over three hundred verses that show God's concern for the poor and other oppressed people.

First Baptist Church in downtown San Francisco is a diverse church not only because of the cultural difference of its members, but also because of its socioeconomic inclusivity. It offers a free Wednesday evening meal and optional Bible study. Low income and homeless attendees show up, but so do single parents, poor seminary students, and concerned church members. A few years ago, it was rare to see many low income and homeless participants at more formal Sunday worship services. When they did attend, most sat in the back corner. Over time, that dynamic shifted. The income dispersion is now evident around the sanctuary. A formerly homeless man leads the cooking, assisted by various church members. Pastor Ryan Blackwell attends dinners, stops to counsel, and conducts open office hours during which anyone is welcome.

The Church Planting Challenge to Start Churches Among the Far People

Most church planting organizations and denominations are willing to acknowledge that North America is a mission field, but it is less common for these organizations to strategize accordingly. On foreign fields, church planters are supported as *missionaries*, but in North America they are supported as *church planters*. Church planters are expected to quickly churn out members, baptisms, and professions of faith. As long as they deliver these things, they are celebrated and supported. On the other hand, most overseas missionary sending agencies make allowances for much slower rates of conversion and church reproduction.

Church planting agencies want immediate results. They are inclined to help with church planting among immigrant Christians who enter North America and quickly gather as new churches, but they are not willing to wait for the planters to make inroads among the more difficult to reach from those cultures. For example, a church planter among South Asians in the United States will draw attention and receive praise, as well as financial support, for starting a Hindi-speaking church among newly arrived Christians from India. However, a church planter toiling among three million other Asian Indians in the country, most of who represent unreached people groups, will produce less immediate results and likely be underappreciated.

Our cross-cultural church planting strategies also need to include a broader assessment process. Emmanuel, from Liberia, feels called to plant a church that reaches newcomers from many countries. He is an intellectual introvert, not at all a stereotypical entrepreneurial American church planter. At first, his denomination questioned his capacity to start a church; however, planting a church with a leader who can reach Africans was too wonderful an opportunity to pass up, so his efforts were supported.

Planting churches among poor people can also be daunting, especially when the churches are traditionally structured. How does a very poor community pay for a pastor's salary and the use of a building, while attempting to become indigenous, self-supporting, and reproducing? Glenn and Linda Greene are starting a church in California's Central Valley among the very poor. They are completely bi-vocational, receive no salary from their church, and use a building that is available to them on Wednesday evenings, but not on Sundays. They launched on January 1, 2012, and ninety people were present for Easter week. Some churches among the poor conduct services out of doors as a church without walls, and some simply continue to multiply churches that meet in homes. CityTeam ministries, based in San Jose, California, recently reproduced 460 churches in sixty-two cities within a period of a few years. Most of these were among the poor and were started and led by poor Christians. Both immigration issues and subsidy to the poor are hot-button political issues that divide good Christians, but here is the challenge. Wherever you stand politically, God has allowed access to people from all over the world who need Christ. There is no mistaking His intent: "Go into all the world and preach the gospel to all creation" (Mk. 16:15). "[A]nd you will be my witnesses in Jerusalem, and in all Judea and Samaria, and to the ends of the earth" (Acts 1:8). And, in the end, "After this I looked, and there before me was a great multitude that no one could count, from every nation, tribe, people and language, standing before the throne and before the Lamb." (Rev.

7:9). There is no doubt that God wants *all* saved, that He has made that more possible now than at any time in history, and that new churches are needed as a response to the harvest God is preparing.

But who will go, and whom is He sending? Reaching the least reached among us will never happen through paid professional church planters who carry on their shoulders the mandate of immediate, measurable results. We will never have enough paid church planters to reach them. This is also true about reaching very poor people. It is not practical or wise to think in terms of fully paid personnel. The only possibility for the task is what my friend Felicity Dale calls "an army of ordinary people."[3] It is therefore critical to equip and mobilize lay mission teams and to think locally and globally about the task of evangelism and church planting.

Chapter 8

Three Tenses of Knowing a Community

LINDA BERGQUIST

God reigns, God has reigned, God shall reign for all eternity. –FROM THE *SHACHARIT*, THE DAILY PRAYER SERVICE OF THE JEWISH PEOPLE

Most church planters who Linda and Allan know are oriented towards the future. They imagine, dream, plan, innovate, and work towards something they believe will be true some day. They learn to write vision statements. Their capacity to communicate their vision effectively to others is considered a major indicator of whether or not they will be able to plant a church. Church planters are also expected to live well in the present tense. They must engage community, develop real relationships, practice evangelism, and live transformational lives. If some choose present tense activities because these things help them to accomplish their future tense objectives, who is checking?

The future/present nature of church planters' work predisposes them towards neglecting a community's past. After all, the two great tasks of the Church today are to do everything it knows how to do to concentrate on its present situation, while at the same time, addressing the future.[1] This chapter is about how the past shapes the present, how present tense experiences and trends shape a church planter and a church's future, and why these things matter to church planters who care enough to really get to know their communities.

A Future Orientation

A Confession from Linda

When my friends read this chapter, some of them will laugh at what I wrote. Church planting strategists like me are often even more future-oriented than the church planters we serve. We regularly think in leapfrog mode, meaning that before we finish one thing, we are ready to leap to the next. We can hardly imagine planting a church and staying with it for the long haul. Even our own big picture stories seem small to us very quickly.

My husband is God's gift to help me live better in the present. Eric is the most incarnational person I know. When my mind flings too far forward, he helps me bring it back home again. I have also learned to appreciate the importance of history and of understanding a community's past tense. San Francisco has been my teacher in this. Her history has wooed me, and her roots have stirred me to believe in her future. While I confess my addiction to the future, at the same time, I am convicted that church planting, like Christian living, is a commitment in three tenses. It is an acknowledgment that our God reigns over time and that time is subject to Him.

The Value of Vision

Linda teaches church planting classes inside of a state prison where a number of inmates have accrued either very long sentences or life imprisonment. Even so, a number of these students have elaborate dreams about ministries and churches they will catalyze some day. They seem to be "good and saved," wholeheartedly in love with Jesus, and eager to make their lives count for the Kingdom. One man, whom we shall call Randy, has sixty years left before he completes his sentence, yet he carries around an outline of a ministry that he is eager to start after he is released. He has even figured out how to come up with the financial resources needed for the task. Are these prisoners visionary thinkers? Maybe a few are, but, most importantly, their love for Christ compels them to imagine and plan towards the future. Great visionary capacity is a remote substitute for a passionate, obedient life in Christ. God Himself is the vision caster. Our role is to join His team, grasp His vision for the Kingdom, and move forward in the power of His Spirit.

Why Church Planters Gravitate Towards the Future

Planters Like Starting Churches in New Communities

Church planters especially like starting churches in large, homogenous new communities. They expect to discover a greater likelihood that at least some people are already looking for a new church home, and think they can more easily convince prospective sponsoring organizations that a new church is needed in the homogenous setting. New neighborhoods do not have much history—no past tense. They do have strong hope for the future. In new cities and towns, church planters are positioned to help create their communities' new realities. They can help shape the cultures of the places where they live, and they offer venues where neighbors can meet one another. In homogenous communities people need to work less diligently at finding common ground and find it easier to forge relationships.

New Churches Become Venues for Shaping the Future

Church plants are often modeled after entrepreneurial business practices. These businesses emphasize the value of newness. New services, new products, new designs, and new strategies are routine. Thinking ahead of the curve is just part of the adventure. Many church plants regularly adopt this ethos along with the future orientation that goes with it.

Church Planters Are Often Young and Most Interested in Reaching Their Own Generation

Large numbers of church planters in the United States and Canada seek to work with people in their own young age bracket. Perhaps the same holds true in other countries too. The church planting world prefers a youthful culture for the above reasons. Starting a church is hard work. By middle age, many people feel like they no longer have the energy for it. Some planters, immersed in the tasks of engaging in mission and addressing the future, choose to plant churches partially because it helps them bypass what they consider the baggage of old church organizations. This seems to be less true for first-generation immigrants than it is for other groups.

Church Planters Are Innovative

Church planters are some of the greatest innovators of the Christian world. They often attempt to press forward into the future by experimenting with new ways of practicing church. Sometimes they make progress, but other times they innovate without really working towards real challenges that innovation can help solve. Roger Martin, dean of the University of Toronto's Rotman School of Management, claims, "For any company that chooses to innovate, the foremost challenge is this... Are you willing to step back and ask, 'What's the problem we're trying to solve?' They take on a mystery, some abstract challenge, and they try to create a solution."[2]

Algorithms, Heuristics, and Mystery

In studying how businesses work, Martin created a framework for addressing this question about what problem needs to be solved. It has interesting implications for the Church as it poses new, but similar, questions. He claims that when an idea, model, or paradigm works well, it functions according to a set of rules, or an *algorithm* that is predictable and acceptable. There is little impetus for change. Sometimes, however, the algorithm stops working without any clear reason why. Martin calls this next stage *mystery*. Eventually, through a discovery process, some clarification emerges, which is called the *heuristic*. Eventually, a new algorithm emerges. Sometimes the design problem requires a minor adjustment, but sometimes a major overhaul is needed. This process may help inform the Church during a time in its history when what once seemed predictable is now much less so.

The tension here is that algorithm is hardwired into God's creation. For life to exist, a certain amount of predictability is necessary. God put universal laws in place that at one time in human history were vast mysteries–gravity, the elements, fire, and photosynthesis, to name a few. He is the Master of many mysteries that will never be unraveled on this side of eternity. Scripture teaches that algorithm and mystery co-exist: "Beyond all question, the mystery from which true godliness springs is great: / He appeared in the flesh, / was vindicated by the Spirit, / was seen by angels, / was preached among the nations, / was believed on in the world, / was taken up in glory" (1 Tim. 3:16). The Christian believes that these truths, which are not fully explainable, are nevertheless credible, believable, and predictable (algorithmic) enough to build one's life on. *The Message* version of the introduction in this same phrase says, "This Christian life is a great mystery, far exceeding our understanding, but some things are clear enough" (1 Tim 3:16a).

Innovative church planters must affirm the critical algorithms that God set in place, but they must also add a lens for perceiving mystery differently. They need critical capacities that help them imagine differently while asking and answering new questions.

Here is one example. In some places in the world, such as Europe and parts of North America, postmodernism changed the culture before the Church knew the concept. The Church's failure to evangelize postmodern peoples effectively remained a mystery until enough people in the Church became aware of the cultural change. The world really was changing. The Church could and needed to begin trying to understand what was happening (heuristic). The Church has experienced much misperception about what seems to be an emerging worldview, and still nobody has really figured it all out. In all this change and confusion it is easier to undertake dealing with a problem that is named than one that is a complete mystery.

Engaging the Present

At its best, planting a church is an incarnational activity. New churches are first conceived in the heart of God, who invites humans to interact with the birthing process. The Spirit nurtures that impulse, and, in the fullness of time, a church comes into being. It is intended to represent the Son, and, like him, actively participate in the world. The Incarnation is about the Son who submitted himself to being born as a human baby, choosing to live on earth as the image of the invisible God. At least two senses of the word *incarnation* apply here. First, the term carries with it the implication that something unseen takes on form. The Word became flesh and lived among humanity as one of us (Jn. 1:14). Wholehearted Christians are persuaded to go ahead–get messy, be human, participate in the present, start a church.

The word *incarnation* or *incarnational* is also used to mean that Christians must give form to their ideas and beliefs about Jesus by engaging in practical and sacrificial ministry to others. Incarnation is about embracing a missional posture and fully acknowledging that "God was reconciling the world to himself in Christ... And he has committed to us the message of reconciliation" (2 Cor. 5:19). To be involved in incarnational ministry demands doing more than inviting people to church or preaching a relevant sermon. It is about embodying Christ by carrying His love into a community in ways that help people become reconciled to God.

Oakland, California, is an earthy and courageous city. It is known for its ethnic diversity, high crime rate, widespread community activism, and grassroots participation in the arts. Its city scene is common, accessible, immediate, and participatory. It suggests that incarnation is real and that it does not observe from the outside. Over the years, many potential church planters we know have explored Oakland's city core. Some rejected Oakland in favor of predictability, and others in favor of mystery. Few have the vision to glory in its juxtaposition of new condominiums, old storefronts, and streets that can be all at once fabulous and filthy. Such a vision requires imagination generous enough to realize that incarnation precedes the salvation and resurrection for which the city of Oakland yearns. Finally, however, the revitalized Oakland we perceived some years ago is getting the attention it deserves. The *New York Times* ran an article in early 2012 about the forty-five places to travel that year. Oakland was number five, right between London and Tokyo.[3] Recently, a church planting team moved into west Oakland. Within a few weeks, one family had a car window shot out during an incident on their street. Incarnation is tough sometimes.

Other cities have to deal with tough neighborhoods like Oakland does—for example, Detroit, New Orleans, and parts of Los Angeles. Church planters are not lining up to move into these cities. Present tense ministry requires sacrifice, and it requires experimentation. It is living in the heuristic. This same thing holds true for church planters, even in much less challenging places. For many, sacrifice is a matter of funding, or living arrangements, or a too full schedule. While some people plan to work another job while starting a church, others experience great surprise at the personal funding problems. Certain of funding, they find it never comes through. Others never intended for their spouses to work full time to pay the bills, but it became a necessity. Some leave behind large homes in one town to discover they can afford half the house in their new community. A church planting team in Tijuana, Mexico, constructed a church building in the pastor's backyard. At any hour of the day or night, church planters dropped in for advice, assistance, or food. A pot of beans and fresh tortillas were always available to them. The founding church pastor and his family not only sacrificed by giving up their backyard, but their living room and kitchen also belonged to Jesus. This wholehearted follower of Jesus had a mission to raise up and send out church planters not only to Tijuana, but also across the border to the United States.

This present tense, exploratory, heuristic way of life makes most church planting a missionary endeavor, even in places where the gospel has a foothold. Like overseas missionaries, church planters often leave behind family, friends, living wages, and comfortable homes. Unless they are indigenous, they also must learn new cultures, new practices, and new ways of sharing Christ. Much of the time, they shoulder financial burdens alone or with minimal assistance. They are strong, courageous, and patient in a highly present tense way; they sacrifice for the sake of the gospel. That's wholeheartedness.

Learning from the Past

Church planters are often newcomers to the places where they start churches. They arrive as protagonists, with a goal of transforming the spiritual climate of their adopted communities. This is admirable, yet often short sighted. "Conquerors are seldom interested in a thoroughgoing discovery of where they are."[4] Thoughtful consideration of a place's past demonstrates wisdom and foresight, but most church planters do not take time to investigate and appreciate the history of a place. Neglecting a place's history is analogous to a physician treating a patient without first gathering a history that helps inform the diagnosis. History can also help uncover unique strengths and reveal the work God has already placed in motion. Many planters define the new church's mission, values, and goals before they even move to their new communities. In new suburbs, this may matter less. However, cities, especially old cities, have unique histories, and each carries with it a story the knowledge of which can truly assist church planters in learning about where they live and work.

Remembrance: A Gift from Old Cities

Followers of Christ are instructed to remember together. Community is strengthened through outward expressions such as rituals, celebrating, feasting, or abstaining that are regularly and relationally observed. They are called to eat the bread and drink the cup together in remembrance of Him (Lk. 22:19; 1 Cor. 11:24). Remembering the Sabbath is to keep it holy (Ex. 20:8). As priest and leader of the Israelites, Samuel created a monument he called an Ebenezer as a visual reminder of God's miraculous saving work on the people's behalf (1 Sam. 7:12). When Israel crossed into the Promised Land, Joshua obeyed God and constructed a memorial in Gilgal out of twelve stones the Israelites had carried across the Jordan (Josh. 4:21–24).

San Francisco, where Linda lives, is an old city with a past worth knowing and remembering. Its history profoundly shapes its present tense reality. It is useful to note that San Francisco has been ethnically diverse for 150 years. Its reputation for sexual promiscuity dates back to the Gold Rush days, not the 1960s. Some of San Francisco's stories are devastating: fires that all but destroyed it (1849–1852 and 1906), the Chinese Exclusion Act (1882–1943) and accompanying prejudice, significant earthquakes (1906 and 1989), the People's Temple mass suicide led by an

Evangelical from San Francisco (November 18, 1978), the assassination of mayor George Moscone and supervisor Harvey Milk just nine days later (November 27, 1978), and the many lives that have been lost as a result of the AIDS epidemic. After the slaying of Moscone and Milk, the *San Francisco Examiner* described San Francisco as "a city with more sadness and despair in its heart than any city should have to bear."[5] Today there are still San Franciscans who remember that the 1978 slayings happened at the hands of professed Christians, and they have kept their vows to never again enter the doors of a church building. How can history inform a church-planting posture and assist planters in reaching cites? In the end, good church planters work with a preferable future in mind, but they have the wisdom to learn from a community's past and compassion enough for people's immediate needs that they minister well in present tense.

Chapter 9

A Team Perspective on Knowing

ALLAN AND KATHY KARR

By the year 2000, the Karr family was deeply entrenched in the church we planted in Castle Rock, Colorado. I (Allan) was also traveling and training people in the start up phase of church plants. By then I was also a professor of church planting at Golden Gate Seminary. Sometimes my wife Kathy would travel with me and teach a segment of the class or training conference designed to encourage the spouses of a church planting team. She developed some excellent material that I have occasionally incorporated into sections of this book as it applies. We focus on her special materials in this chapter. Kathy originally entitled her presentation, "12 Challenges for the Spouses in a Church Planting Team."[1] Later she amended it for a different context for spouses of a bi-vocational[2] church planting team. Her practical insights help church planters, team members, and family to understand how to be wholehearted in knowing God, knowing yourself, knowing your macrocommunity, and knowing your microcommunity. This practical advice was gleaned from Kathy's role in our church planting team and came from insights she has gained as a spouse in team ministry as we served together for over twenty-seven years. We discovered that "knowing" is integral to loving. She makes a clear distinction between the leadership role of an existing church and the role in a church planting team. I have taken Kathy's material and woven in my own commentary, but I am honored she allowed me to include her ideas in this work.

Challenges for a Wholehearted Church Planting Team

When Kathy is speaking to team members, it is often mostly to women. Some church cultures maintain a very strong gender distinction when it comes to roles in ministry. Our perspective is that the phrase "church planter" is gender neutral. All over the world, the majority of missionaries are women, and many of them carry the mission assignment of being "church planters." I have designed creative positions in the United States for my students who are female and feel called to church planting. My co-author, Linda, has been a church planter for decades, and a church planting catalytic leader for most of that time. That said, these challenges are for everyone on the church planting team, but we wanted to address the women particularly, so they are affirmed as integral and valuable. Everyone on the team, including the spouse, is called to be wholehearted, and these are very practical ways of knowing people (and along the way God and yourself).

Challenge 1: Verify a Strong Sense of Call

This material is addressed to the church planting team (rather than "Challenges for Church Planter Wives") for a definite reason. Kathy says, "You are not the wife of a church planter; rather you are the wife (the female) in a church planting team. This is a great commitment for both you and your husband, and you need to be and feel called to it just as he is." Church planting is a team effort, and everyone on the team is a large part of what will happen, either positive or negative. This challenge is not model specific. A labor and resource intensive model of church planting will include being full-time vocationally. Similarly, a relational church planting model also requires you earn your family income in a vocation beyond the church leadership roles. The calling in your life is foundational to being wholehearted. The needs of the people will not keep you on the field in times of discouragement, but your calling will. No matter what model of church you are planting, wholehearted church planters need to feel a strong sense of calling, a sense that you can't do anything else and still be obedient to God. Everyone on the team faces the challenge to be empowered by a personal sense of calling to the people where the church is being planted.

Challenge 2: Keep a Close Personal Relationship with God

You may say, yes, of course, we know this already. This is too basic (and we already covered this in a previous chapter). But in case this is the only chapter of the book you read, you need to know this is the most important thing in your life. Everything that you do and who you are depends upon your relationship with the Lord–this includes your family, your friendships, and the church that God has called you to plant.

We cannot do God's work unless He is accomplishing it through us. We are to be His vessels. Without a continual close relationship with Him, you cannot accomplish what He has set before you. The church God has called you to plant needs God, His plan, His vision, His people–it requires His breath of life, the power of His Spirit.

In John 15:5, Jesus says that we are the branches and, to bear fruit, we must be connected to Him, the vine. Jesus then adds the phrase, "Apart from me you can do *nothing*" (emphasis added). The fruit is real Kingdom work, which is work God is doing through us as His vessels. A lot of work that is called "ministry" is not Kingdom work because it is done "apart from

Him." It is done through a reliance on our own personalities and strengths. It looks good! Beautiful treasures (in man's eyes) are built by some Christian ministries. However, anything apart from Him is *nothing.* In Matthew 6:19, Jesus says in His "Sermon on the Mount," "Do not store up for yourselves treasures on earth, where moth and rust destroy, and where thieves break in and steal" (NASB). In speaking for God, Amos 5:26–27 says God will send His people into exile for things "you made for yourselves" (NASB). We can get so caught up in "doing ministry" that we forget that God is not impressed. In Amos 5:21–23, God criticizes some things we might think are good things for a church plant, or any church for that matter:

> I hate, I reject your festivals,
> Nor do I delight in your solemn assemblies.
> Even though you offer up to Me burnt offerings
>   and your grain offerings,
> I will not accept *them*;
> And I will not even look at the peace offerings
>   of your fatlings.
> Take away from Me the noise of your songs;
> I will not even listen to the sound of your harps. (NASB)

God was not impressed with the worship services, offerings, and songs when they were done with a heart that was less than whole. God even said He hates and rejects them and won't even listen to the songs of praise. The prophet spoke strongly the truth of God's heart on this issue.

We need to listen to hear what is His work and obey His will. Church planting offers more freedom to *do* His work because you have fewer existing ministries to keep juggling. John 15:5 gives us a promise: if we remain in Jesus, we *will* bear much fruit. What is one of the main things that is needed to keep this relationship alive and close? Jesus says you have not because you ask not. We have to be in constant prayer so that our work is His work done through us. We can't do what He has called us to do if we aren't letting Him do it through us.

Kathy points out that some people say or think, "Well, God knows everything happening in my life. I don't need to pray for Him to respond." Our response is, Why, then, did *Jesus* pray? And why does He, over and over, tell *us* to pray? God does work and respond to the prayers of His people. Ask others to pray for you too. Prayer is a communication line to God that is vital to wholehearted church planting.

Stay in His Word regularly, and keep regular times of devotional reading. This takes discipline, time, and effort, but don't let your busyness and other pressures push this out. This is most essential to your life and your church plant.

We encourage you to remember your first love, to keep your relationship with Christ fresh and alive. When is the easiest time to neglect your relationship with God? When you are busy and discouraged. When you serve, if it becomes a chore to you then your ministry has become a job, not a calling. If you enjoy it, it is a ministry. In general, you need more enjoyment than chores. God is the one who can keep your joy present. Your ministry has to come out of your love for the Lord or else you may find yourself resenting the church. This is not fun. Psalm 16:11 says, "You will make known to me the path of life; / In Your presence is fullness of joy; / In Your right hand there are pleasures forever" (NASB). Understanding this challenge is key to wholehearted church planting.

Challenge 3: Remember That It Is God's Church and His Plan

In Numbers 13, the Israelites were doing reconnaissance in the land God promised to them.. Numbers 13:33 explains how the spies felt like grasshoppers when they saw the "giants" who inhabited the land. They had forgotten how big God is by comparison. Wholehearted planters keep our eyes on God and not the circumstances.

In a similar passage, Matthew 14:29–31, Peter tried to walk to Jesus on the water. As long as Peter kept his eyes on Jesus (the truth), he succeeded. When he put his eyes on the circumstances (the storm, wind, and waves), he sank–he failed in what Jesus told him to do. Why? These two stories have a similar principle. Fear set in when the characters' focus was not on the Lord but on themselves. They couldn't accomplish the goal with only their own strength and the circumstances. The Israelites and Peter got scared; they cowered and sank–failed. Wholehearted church planters keep their eyes on God and what He can do.

What is "success"? This principle hits home when church planters begin to define success in their church plant. Remember, success is not limited to numbers: in our culture, churches are often encouraged to count "noses and nickels." How many baptisms? How many in are in attendance? How many dollars were given in offerings? God has many other measurements of success, in *addition* to these things. These statistics *can* be helpful in communicating how a church plant is doing, but they can be very destructive if church planters limit their sense of value only to these criteria. It is easy to begin to focus in on these *things* instead of focusing in on the Lord, who is sovereign and who is in control of these things anyway. If we get caught up in the numbers game, are we questioning God and His sovereignty? God has a Kingdom perspective and His ways are not our ways.

Jesus exemplified this. Following our success criteria, He had so much more that He *could* have accomplished on earth. Jesus often withdrew from crowds. He died at age thirty-three in the prime of His ministry. He never planted a church. With his human criteria and expectations, Peter (in his flesh) fought against God's plan for Jesus' life. Yet when Jesus died, He said, "It is finished."[3] Jesus' work on earth was *complete*. He had done all that the Father had planned.

What happens in your church plant (if you are faithful) is up to God. Don't let the world's opinion of success affect your accomplishment of God's plan for your life. Psalm 46:10 says, "Cease *striving* and know that I am God" (NASB). Just be faithful to Him and *obey*.

God is the source of the increase and not ourselves (even with all the wonderful things we have to offer). We need to rest in His outcome. Always remember: God brings the people and causes the growth in His timing. Expect good things, but do not get so discouraged if God works in ways you had not envisioned. God has a plan, and there may be reasons why things are as they are. God may be building a solid structure, a biblical identity of the church, or personal growth in the planting team.

We really had to come to grips with this a few years back. We would seem to get stuck or plateau at certain attendance numbers. We wondered why we weren't growing any faster. We would begin pressing to find out, "How many did we have today?" and other similar questions. This began taking precedence over people's needs, relationships, and what God desired to accomplish. Maybe this was not true so much outwardly, but our spirits felt it.

You know, God has a plan…maybe if we had grown faster our structure would not have been solid enough to handle it. We had a lot of new Christians, so maybe they would have gotten too caught up in service to maintain the organization and wouldn't have been able to grow spiritually as they should. Maybe the church leadership was not strong or mature enough, or maybe those involved would have gotten too burned out, or maybe we would have become too prideful.

Warning: Beware of the temptation to make comparisons.[4] When you compare yourself, your spouse, or your church with others, it leads to one of two things (or sometimes both), and both are negative:

1. *Pride.* If your church numbers compare favorably to others, you inwardly think, "We are better than they are." The Bible speaks to this issue over and over. If we are honest, we know that we have had moments of pride for things that only rob credit from God.
2. *Feelings of discouragement and failure.* If you compare yourself to other church plants, eventually your church will fall short in the objective measures of success. Then you begin to struggle inwardly with a sense of failure. Most church planters share a common inward fear, the fear of failure. Usually the failure we fear is one whose standards are set by worldly standards rather than biblical ones.

Finally, when your church does grow and becomes more established, make sure that you continue the things that got you started in the first place. The plowing (prayer) and the sowing of the gospel seeds are so important. A wholehearted church planter will not be content to only train existing Christians (those who already know Him). If your church does nothing more than all the whole Body does, your church will spiritually plateau. More importantly, God reaches people through your prayers and your sharing of the gospel. God is about reaching people to know Him and wants us to be His vessels in this endeavor. It is part of our blessing.

Challenge 4: Be Prepared to Minister Outside of Your Expertise, Comfort Zone, Specific Calling, and Preferences

Existing churches have people already in place to do most of the various ministries and program needs. Are you naturally one to help your spouse a lot or one to sit on the sidelines and do only what is fun to you? Go into church planting with a mind to work, and not always in your comfort zones.

In the initial phases of a church plant, the human resources are limited. As a member of a church planting team, you will find the new church will need your help–gifts, skills, time, and encouragement. If you can't or won't do it, important tasks often won't happen. Sometimes God will lead you to wait for His person to accomplish certain things, but sometimes God says you're the one and you need to step up to the plate!

God can use this to stretch us and grow us. Many things you will help to do will be out of your comfort zone, or you may not prefer to do them. However, if God leads you to do them, *obey* and He will bless your efforts in His way. Second Corinthians 12:9 says, "My grace is sufficient for you, for power is perfected in weakness" (NASB). The best thing is when we feel weak, we know who is doing the work. God has gifted and enabled you in every way that is needed for you to accomplish *His* purpose *if* you're willing to say "Yes!" to Him.

There may be Sundays when you help set up, teach a class, greet, and work in the nursery, and then help tear down. Usually the church plant has no paid administrative assistant at the church, so part of that may fall on you. You might fill many needs: phone calls, counseling, hosting people in your home, office work, and many other tasks. It is normal that this may all be a part of a church plant. Wholehearted church planters gear up for this season in their lives. Along the way you may discover some new gifts and passions. Be ready for this exciting season of your life on a church planting team.

Challenge 5: Know That Your Home Life Will Be More Hectic

In the initial phase of our first church plant, Kathy's mom came to our home for a short visit. At that point, the church office was in our basement, including the church phone. People were in and out of our home all day long. Both phones, church and home (this was before every family member had cell phones), were ringing constantly.

Every day was busy with church activities, and our home was the center of the beehive of activity, a revolving door with people in and out.

Kathy's mom was shocked and appalled at the busyness of our lives and our home. She exclaimed over and over again that she had no idea that church planting was so hectic and all-consuming. She was used to living a quiet, secluded life that was "busy" if she had an appointment and a phone call each day. She quickly realized the start up phase of a church plant is a very hectic season of life.

Life becomes even more hectic if your church office is in your home, as was true with us. Our church-planting budget made the cost of renting an office space out of the question. For the first time in our ten-year marriage, Allan was at home *all the time!* This was truly wonderful *and* a challenge at the same time. Allan was used to having lots of administrative assistants, so he was constantly pounding up the stairs, yelling, "*Kath, Kath,* where is (this or that)?" or looking for some other assistance. With the church office in your home, it's difficult to get away from the phone, fax, and copy machine. There is always something that needs to be done.

Another aspect adding to our hectic life is that we are very hospitable. We have historically had lots of guests stay in our home. Our method of church planting and ministry is very relational. Because of our team strategy, the first years of planting we had overnight guests in our home 200–250 of the 365 days of the year. When you live in Colorado, lots of people want to visit you. That doesn't include all the dinner and dessert people with whom we were developing friendships, or the small groups and church meetings that met in our home in the evenings. The challenge is this: in a church plant, your home life will likely be a very hectic season of your church life.

What could help your home life in this situation? If possible, consider having a separate church office. Be creative. Ask a local church or business to support your church plant by giving you a room to use as a church office in your start up phase. If at first you must have the church office in your home, then use phones that can be muted after hours. Additionally, find other venues for church meetings and appointments with people. Use coffee shops or other homes to have meetings, whenever possible. This spreads out the hecticness to other team members.

Other ideas for setting boundaries are discussed in depth in the chapter on loving yourself appropriately. However, one benefit of this busy home: we let our children get involved, so they felt like it was their ministry too. Our children have loved the overnight guests, the people in the mission groups, and the dinner guests. As small children they had fun helping mail out flyers, paint, stuff envelopes, and set up on Sunday mornings. Let your children feel like they are a big part of it, because in reality they are. Our two older children who remember our first church plant have extremely fond memories of the friendship and communitas we experienced in that season. In our second church plant, a more relational model, the memories are rich and sweet, and they are still being made.

Challenge 6: Expect Times of Discouragement

Our spiritual lives have their ups and downs. In the same way, our church life has seasons and stages. Some are challenging and even quite difficult. Some are fun, celebrative, and exciting. Understand that the highs are higher and the lows are lower in church planting. These two extremes seem to be even more pronounced in a church plant due to the emotional toll, church growth issues, and the health and stability of the church.

The best advice we received came from a peer church planter when we arrived on the mission field. He said, "Church planting is like a roller coaster—get ready for the ride." This advice helped us because, when on a high and then low, his words came back to our memory, letting us know this was normal in church planting.

Some Sundays we would come home so excited, and some days we were very discouraged. Our first church plant was an attractional model, and worship leadership was such a challenge for our church plant. Music was a large part of our identity, and we could never seem to find someone who matched our vision and hopes for leading corporate worship times. We remember plateaus when it seemed we were stuck at certain levels of attendance. Holidays were so hard at first. When you don't have very many attending, a few more people gone on a holiday Sunday makes a big difference.

Our Colorado culture was challenging as well. We lived in a giant playground, summer and winter. In that culture, people head to the mountains every chance they get. Additionally, all the little league sports in our city were on Sunday mornings. Additionally, people in Colorado get transferred so frequently that it seemed you'd finally get strong leadership in place, and then they would announce they had been transferred in their job to another city. The average time to reside in our city was around two years, so we used to say we had to grow really fast just to break even. In our model of church this was often very discouraging.

In church life and our spiritual life, we are constantly trying to level out the highs and lows. It seems to be a constant process. This leads to a need to guard against weariness, negative attitudes and emotions, and discouragement. Galatians 6:9 says, "So let's not allow ourselves to get fatigued doing good. At the right time we will harvest a good crop if we don't give up, or quit"(*The Message*).Wholehearted church planters understand the challenge of discouraging moments and seasons, and rely on God to give them the strength to be resilient.

Challenge 7: Expect to Experience Feelings of Isolation and Loneliness

Church planting is different from being the pastor of an existing church. When you make a decision to move to a new job at an existing church, you normally find immediate support and a friendship base to draw upon. We usually had the new church assist us with our move, unloading the truck, cleaning, and organizing, and often coming into our new home with fresh home-cooked meals and filling the pantries with groceries. When church planting, you often have nobody but your family at first. If you are blessed, your team will be there for you. We remember struggling to unload our moving truck and waking up the next morning to realize that, while we believed we had moved to a new town to pastor a new church, the truth was that the new church only existed in the vision of our imagination. The whole church was sleeping under the one roof of our home.

Additionally, for whatever reason, the people who do commit initially to a church plant are not always people you're naturally drawn to or enjoy. It takes even longer to establish close friendships, and you can tend to feel somewhat lonely. Sometimes it just takes a while for God to bring one of those very special friends along that you really feel like you connect with.

The question is: What are some things you can do that will help you in this reality? One key—maintain a strong marriage relationship because you need to be able to draw on each other for friendship and support. My spouse is my best friend, and our relationship was a tremendous help in easing some of these early negative feelings. Work extra hard on your marriage relationship prior to and during church planting. If you don't enjoy your spouse, you may feel even more totally isolated.

We had a great sponsoring church that was a tremendous support. They didn't interfere, tell us what to do, or complain. They were great encouragers in any and every way—including funding, equipment, and prayer support. However, one of the biggest things our sponsors did was offer *smiles* and *friendliness*. They arranged church planters wives' lunches 3–4 times each year, during which they took the women out to lunch at a nice restaurant while providing childcare. The wives could talk, gripe, be encouraged, or whatever they needed.

This is one of the great advantages of "the network." We will discuss this in greater detail in a later chapter, but the network assists when the team is feeling isolated. We encourage teams to take advantage of any of these opportunities, even if you don't think you need it—it helps in long run.

Finally, in times of isolation and loneliness, we need to remember the great biblical truth. In Matthew 28:20, Jesus said, "I am with you always, to the very end of the age." Wholehearted church planters remind themselves daily that we live in communion with the community of the Trinity. The Father, Son, and Holy Spirit are omnipresent in every moment of our lives. Being aware that feelings of isolation and loneliness are normal and real, we trust in the spiritual reality that we are not alone. We can take steps to make sure we have support with skin on.

Challenge 8: Know That You May Have a Heavier Decision-Making Role

In the initial stages of a church plant the lead planter and the team have no elders, deacons, staff, or even—sometimes—friendship support. Consequently, a lot of weight falls on every member of the team, if they accept it. You have to make decisions about program structure, meeting places, timing, colors, logos, worship leaders, general direction, by-laws, mailers/marketing, budget, and countless details. Literally hundreds of decisions must be made, depending on the church plant model. Basically, you get to make the decisions. This can be fun, but it is an added challenge and burden.

Being the decision-maker brings up a question: If you do accept greater decision-making and you like it, what struggle in your life are you going to face as the church grows, creating new structural changes and calling on you to share or surrender your role as a decision maker? As team members, we pray for God to raise up new leaders from the harvest. When God does raise up church leadership, pray that you will know when it's time to back off, and how. The challenge is to be ready to give away the responsibility to make decisions in the new season of church planting. It's not only biblical, but it is also healthy for you and the church body.

Kathy would admit that after being so involved in the initial season of decision making *and liking it*, when God did raise up leaders at our new church and they began functioning and making decisions, that she felt left out and frustrated. Allan would come home from an organizational meeting of some kind and not be in the mood to rehash all that took place, so Kathy felt left out of what she had originally been such an integral part. It was especially hard when their decisions weren't exactly what she would have decided.

Finding your role in the next stage of the church may be harder than starting the church. This most often means the time for the church planter to leave the church and the city. You have to remember that the decisions of that church are no longer your concern or your business. After you leave, the church will do things that you don't agree with. Even more challenging, some people will still try to make the church remain your business. In this season, wholehearted church planters have to adjust their own hearts to live in the season where the decisions of the church are no longer theirs to make.

Challenge 9: Know That You'll Get Tired

Ecclesiastes 3 proves true in every context, but particularly in church planting. "There is an appointed time for everything... A time to give birth and a time to die; / A time to plant and a time to uproot what it planted."[5] Understand that life—particularly ministerial life—has seasons. The one you're in will at the moment will have times of weariness and stress. Kathy grew up on a farm in the Midwest where spring and fall were very busy seasons because of planting and harvesting. She tells of how her family would be up very early and go to bed very late, which would often make for a short season of being very tired. However, you knew that when the crop was in or out you'd have time to rest. We did rest, too, because we knew another busy season was just around the corner. This challenge includes planning and delegating during the busy seasons until the winter rest comes. The follow-up challenge is to back off and rest when you are able to in a new season.

The 80 Percent Rule. In our church planting we use the 80 percent rule: When someone comes along whom you perceive can do what you do 80 percent as well as you, delegate the responsibility to them if they are willing. They often end up doing it better than you if given a chance, in part because it is their focus. They'll be fresher at it than you would when it is not your priority.

Counter the tiredness by walking in the grace life. Understand God's will is for you to minister and be a church planter. While you may get tired, it is not God's will for you to be burned out and suffer physical effects. Matthew 11:28 states: "Come to Me, all who are weary and heavy-laden, and I will give you rest" (NASB). God is your source of peace and inner rest. Listen to what He is telling you.

Challenge 10: Keep a Positive Attitude

Speaking very bluntly, church planting is very hard most of the time, and sometimes painful. Those considering being team members in a church plant need to know this and decide now if you can handle it. If you're not basically emotionally healthy right now, you may need to take time first to get healthy before you attempt to plant a church.

Additionally, you need to remember in the seasons when it does get tough that "*this too shall pass*"[6] (just like the various stages of raising children). When you are tired, discouraged, or your joy is shaky, your thinking is usually off. Remember this, and follow these tips:

- Try not to let your mind wander into areas it shouldn't go.
- Don't overreact to things.
- Avoid pity parties and attitudes like, "I'm the only one committed and laboring for the Lord." Such attitudes are not productive. (To gain perspective, remember that many Christians have actually died for the Lord.)
- Choose to be quiet at times like these. Ecclesiastes 3:7b says there is "a time to be silent and a time to speak." It is often wise to be silent until you get on top of a negative attitude. It doesn't edify anyone to speak contagious, cancerous words.
- If you need to talk, be very careful where you share your discouragement. A church plant is too fragile to handle negative attitudes.

Each team member will be in a position to know and be involved in everything—the positive and the negative. Some events and decisions may seem negative or frustrating to you when they are actually just normal to church planting. Regardless, negative attitudes and grumbling are contagious (just as positive attitudes are). All churches, but especially church plants, are very fragile. A little negativity spreads quickly and can do a lot of damage. Church plants tend to have more times of discouragement than an older, well-established church. Such negativity can literally destroy the church.

We strongly urge you to commit to keeping negative attitudes and frustration and discouragement to yourself, or at least outside of your core group and community. If you need someone to vent to, you might seek out someone totally outside of the church. Sometimes you can share it with your spouse, but sometimes he or she gets discouraged too. We need to encourage our spouses.

My (Kathy's) two sources of support were our monthly Church Planter Network group and the church planter wives' luncheons at our sponsoring church. In the season of our first church plant, I organized a support system for the wives. There were luncheons for the spouses, dinners with speakers, thrift store shopping, and mini-conferences. (Each spouse spoke on topics such as "Crisis," "Criticism," "Conflict," etc.) As much as possible, serve with a joyful heart. It is the characteristic of being wholehearted.

Challenge 11: Be Your Spouse's #1 Supporter and Fan

This is truly a section for the wife of a church planting team. The principles in this challenge come from Kathy Karr, who has ministered with me for twenty-seven years at this point. Kathy knows all my warts and has seen my worst days. Wholehearted church planters have really responded to this challenge throughout the years as Kathy has presented it. Listen to this wisdom from Kathy Karr, a wholehearted church planter...

How many times have you heard what you would consider a bad sermon from your husband? Have you ever responded negatively to this bad sermon? How did he respond to your attitude? Even if he has a bad sermon or if the church is not going as you hoped it would, be supportive. Encourage where you can—*or be quiet!* If your husband feels good about who he is, he'll do a better job anyway. We all have faults and failures, and you know your spouse's faults and failures better than anyone. You also know what buttons to push to get a response. Don't push his buttons even when you're tempted to. He may be discouraged, and this makes it worse.

Whether church planting or serving as a pastor of an existing church, your husband takes a lot of criticism. Although you are in it together, he is going to feel the ultimate weight and burden (in our culture the "buck" usually stops with him). I (Kathy) didn't realize this at first. When I would gripe or complain or get frustrated with how it was going, Allan would get discouraged and take it personally. There's definitely a time to be quiet and say nothing, even with your husband. He is then able to go on and do an even better job because he is not so discouraged. If husbands feel encouragement and support from you, it makes the other criticism much easier to take.

Sidebar: How is your marriage? Many people decide to have a baby to try to strengthen or save their marriage. Does this work? Usually it does not, but why? Because it causes more stress, allowing even less time to face and work out problem issues; being squeezed only magnifies the unresolved issues that were already present.

The same is true in planting a church. Everyone has normal marital struggles, but if you have some pretty good struggles in your marriage, church planting will only magnify those struggles. I urge you to go so far as to even consider postponing the church plant to give yourselves time to work these issues out before you begin. This doesn't mean you won't plant a church, but you may need to wait for different timing, for a healthier season in your life and marriage. The last thing you want is a broken marriage. If your marriage fails, you can't pastor or plant a church in the middle of these struggles anyway. A failed marriage will forever be an obstacle to your life and ministry. Many lives, human resources, and financial resources go into a church plant, so having a healthy marriage is crucial to church planting. It is one characteristic of wholehearted church planters.

Challenge 12: Have Fun!!

Church planting is often difficult and exhausting, especially the season of launching. For some church planters, it may be something God only asks a family to do once. Kathy and I want to encourage you as you begin your churches to remember it's a season and that, regardless of the difficulties and challenges that come up in planting a church, "this too shall pass." You've been called to this, God has equipped you with all you need, and God will bless your efforts when your heart is in line with His heart and will. In spite of the difficulties, Kathy said, "I really had a ball. This was the most fun, challenging, interesting, and rewarding thing I've ever done in the ministry." We pray that it will be the same for each wholehearted church planter and that you will have fun while you're doing it. When we loaded up the moving van and caravanned across the country to plant our first church in Castle Rock, Colorado, we considered it a great adventure. It was, in many more ways than we could have imagined. If you are reading this, it is likely that church planting is part of your life in some way now, or will be in the future. Just have a great time! Wholehearted people have fun lives!

Chapter 10

Loving Your Microcommunity

ALLAN KARR

My happiest moments of my life have been the few which I have passed at home in the bosom of my family. —THOMAS JEFFERSON

What Is Microcommunity?

In the first book Linda and I wrote together, we introduced the term "microcommunity" into the working vocabulary of the church-planting context. In that book, "microcommunity" was defined as:

> [That] which includes the people nearest to us: family, intimate friends, mentors, teammates, and those with whom we share a close community of faith. These are the peoples God uses most frequently to shape us and teach us... By using the term *microcommunity*, we aim to suggest the wealth and beauty of intimate relationship that is difficult to capture in words.[1]

The first critical arena of loving people is the church planter's capacity to love and nurture those who are in the closest spheres of influence: his or her microcommunity. Loving your microcommunity is also about the church planter's capacity to help this community learn to love one another and to bring out the best in them individually and collectively. This includes family, the church planting team, close friends, and others with whom the church planter shares life most intimately. Being a wholehearted person includes living in a way such that one treasures the microcommunity and learns to demonstrate love to them in ways that edify everyone in relationship together.

Relationships, Not Geography

Microcommunity is defined by the closeness of the relationship, not merely the proximity of geography. A person across the ocean can be in your

74

microcommunity because of the love you share, but someone who lives next door could relatively be a stranger and not part of your microcommunity. Many Americans have been raised to be rugged individualists. In our dominant culture, the needs of the individual often have precedence over the needs of the community. In many global cultures, the need of the community is the focus over the need of the individual. Those cultures typically highly value loving their microcommunity. Wholehearted church planters have much to learn from cultures that value the community. It is biblical. Jesus was very good at modeling a Kingdom culture that was not focused on the individual's needs and rights.

About twelve years ago I started traveling much more extensively to international destinations as part of my mission and ministry. A big part of the way that I am wired is that relationships are very important to me. I discovered that my openness to give love freely and receive love freely was well received–right from my first day somewhere–in many cultures where I was a virtual stranger. In a relatively short amount of time, my "family" grew. Whenever I spend two weeks in a place, I inevitably leave there with a bigger microcommunity. I literally have people all over the world who call me their brother (in the family sense, not just the "Christianese" reference), their uncle, their nephew, and even their son. I also have many loved ones who call me "Papa, "Bapak," "Ta Pa," etc., in the context of a godfather, or surrogate father, in respect to the kind of relationship we share. I have many children throughout the world that I have been asked to name by their families, and even some that were named after me, and even after my family members. I have been adopted into many families, into many tribes, and as an honorary member of many churches and villages. I have microcommunity all over the world. Not a day goes by that I don't get an e-mail from some small corner of the globe from a loved one who is a part of my life. I am honored to be considered by them to be part of their lives. My growing understanding of the treasure of the concept of microcommunity has made me feel much richer. I have the most beautiful wife and children, and I would be one of the richest men in the world if my microcommunity were limited strictly to them. However, as I give love to others and receive love from others, I have noticed that God's Spirit has given me a greater capacity to love and more love to give to others in my life. Some of my microcommunity is nearby geographically, but more of it numerically is far away in the context of proximity–but not in heart ties.

Loving Your Family Is Prioritizing Them with Your Time

Working parents in our culture use a popular phrase: "quality time." The implication is that a parent is bombarded by the demands of life and career, and that time with children is limited. To ease their conscience on this tension, they will say, "Well, I spend 'quality time' with my children and family." More than a grain of truth may lie in that statement. We as church leaders/workers need to spend not only "quality time" but a quantity of time as well.

Sometimes we tend to learn the most important lessons of life in painful ways. Maybe we need the pain for our attention to become less focused on our own strategies and more focused on the grace of God and the better life He has in mind for us. Early in my ministry, God graciously taught me the importance of loving my family. I was the pastor of a community church in a small town in the "Bible Belt." The church was growing. People were coming to Christ, joining the church, and being baptized. As a young minister, I was very encouraged. My "success" drove me to work harder and harder. I continually received compliments for the "success" of the church and for being such a hard worker. These remarks drove me to put in more and more time doing "God's work." The apparent fruit justified my workload. Being seen as a successful pastor stroked my ego.

One day, my wife Kathy called me in the middle of the day in my church office. I lived in the "pastorium" (a home for the pastor on the church property), so I was a thirty-second walk from my office to my home. My wife said to me, "Allan, I would like to make an appointment with you."

Stunned and not knowing what to say, I mumbled, "What do you mean?"

Kathy replied, "I need an appointment. Put it on your calendar. If it isn't on your calendar, then something else will come up, and you will need to go. I want to talk to you, and I need it to be on your calendar."

She wasn't being snippy, just sincere. I am sometimes a slow learner in relational things, but she had my attention. I said, "I'll be right there." At home, I quickly discovered she had thought about some things she wanted to say to me. She said, "I have been keeping track of the time you have been working for about a month. You have been averaging over 100 hours per week of 'working at the church.' I know you are excited about the success of the church, but our family needs some of your time. Your calendar is out of balance."

Well, a week has 168 hours. Some of those I sleep, shower, and do small chores, but for the majority of waking hours, I had been doing church work: office time, committees, visitation of prospects and evangelism, outreach, counseling, worship services, preparation for programs, etc. At that time we had two small children. Kathy's words shocked me. My children only saw their dad coming and going, at a distance like another person in the congregation. I was actually showing more love to some in the congregation than I was showing to my family.

Kathy said, "Allan, you will be the pastor to these people for a season of your life. Quite likely we will feel called to move to another place of service someday. But we will be your family *for the rest of your life!* We need a husband and a dad."

She was kind in her correction; but I heard it, and she was right. I later had to relearn this lesson as it applied to the ministry of church planting. The activities of planting will tempt a planter to get time priorities out of balance.

The calendar problem plagues ministers, especially in the dominant church culture. We operate in ways unintentionally damaging to the way we show love to our family. We would love to believe that we are "making disciples." Discipleship in the dominant church culture has often degenerated into making more committed church members who are working hard to build and maintain the organization of the church. New members are groomed to discover their gifts, and then work hard in the various ministries of the church, many of which are quite inward focused as opposed to ministry to the community or giving attention to those who need the truth of the gospel. "Commitment" is measured by the amount of time the leader or team member is working at the church. The pastors and leaders often project these expectations to new Christians and to the other members of the church, even their own families. Ministers' wives either feel neglected or feel an expectation to work as hard as the spouse.

One incident constantly reminds me how sometimes the way we have led, discipled, and lived is not always congruent to showing love to our families. I used to pastor a medium size church in the "Bible Belt" culture. The church was growing with many programs and lots of busy activity at the church. I became close friends with David, an officer in the military who became very loyal to me as pastor. He was also very gifted and had lots of energy. He was my "go to" guy.

If I needed something done, I tended to ask David, in part because I enjoyed his company. I had great confidence and trust he would see the job completed and done well. He rarely said "no" to any request, mostly because he was showing love and loyalty to me. We were busy almost every night of the week together (remember, he had a demanding full-time job in the military). Sundays (even the evening) and Wednesdays were full of church programs and services. The rest of the evenings were full with committee meetings, deacon meetings (David became a deacon), softball and basketball games (we had church teams in the leagues), building/remodeling projects on the church building, visitation/outreach, and various other activities.

David was married with two daughters. At that time I had three small children. One day David confided to me that his marriage was struggling. In exploring the issue, we discovered that a big issue was that David was so busy at "church" and career that he was not home enough to nurture his marriage relationship. David was a really "godly" man based on the way we tended to measure that and evidenced by his commitment and hard work for the church. However, I had great consternation because David was a loyal friend and church member, and I realized I was asking him to commit to a lifestyle that was not being loving to his wife and children. In truth, I wasn't doing much better with my own family. Many women in that culture were hoping their husband would be committed to God, but ironically in that church culture such commitment too often made them less attentive to loving their family because they were never home giving love to the families.

I discovered David wasn't alone. Many leaders in my churches in that season of my life were in the same situation. Sometimes the way we have done ministry and defined "commitment to God" has not been conducive to being loving to our families. "PKs" (Pastor's Kids) have had a notorious reputation for being rebellious or at the very least mischievous. Perhaps they resent the church because it dominated their parents' attention during the years they were growing up. By the time my children were in the heart of their developmental years, we were involved in a different model of church that was more conducive to giving attention to our relationships. Remember, many people can give leadership to a church or a church plant, but only one person can be the mom or dad to your children, or be the spouse to your wife or husband. Wholehearted church planters give their families priority in their lives.

Loving the Microcommunity Virtually

Being "loving" to your microcommunity can be defined in many ways:

1. spending time
2. giving attention to relationships
3. not taking their love for granted
4. working hard to be edifying
5. giving compliments
6. offering genuine prayers voiced intercessionally
7. many other ways.

In this chapter, I have articulated the need for these things. However in this day and age, we need to adapt to the realities of a microcommunity that is global in proximity and learn to use the technology of social networking to express our love.

As I am writing this book, my immediate family is all spread out. My oldest two children are married and live in other states. I have several children in college, even out of state. One of my sons is considering military service. Much of my microcommunity lives in other countries, some even serving in the capacity as missionaries. I am not the most "techie" person on the planet, or even in that category. I am learning to show love with e-mail, social network websites, and even texting, snap-chatting and cell phones. I don't prefer this format, but I actually think my children and their generation do prefer it. We have had holidays where everyone was home, and we were all in the living room with our laptops open and doing our own things. Even in the same room, people are chatting, texting, and Facebook-commenting into each other's conversations. *We were in the same room!* The generation of my children loves to connect with each other, and the use of technology is an important part of it.

If it weren't for e-mail, cell phones, and the Internet, my ability to connect to people would be limited to geographic proximity. Every day I check my e-mail multiple times with my computer and my cell phone. Every text or e-mail from my children or my godchildren brings a smile to my face. I read them immediately and try to respond in a timely manner, with a much greater sense of urgency than I do with e-mails from different contexts. My children love to text with cell phones to connect. I am not passionate about this form of communication. My generation used the telephone. I have had telephones up to my head most of my life–even before there were cell phones. In one of my pastoriums, I am embarrassed to say, I even had a landline installed in my bathroom so I would not miss a call. My two prayer partners are my age or older, so we use the cell phone to connect in our daily prayer discipleship. Even those relationships are dependent on the technology of the cell phone to be the rich spiritual resource they are in our lives.

I recently taught a class in Cameroon to indigenous pastors. I developed some close friendships there, and several wanted to keep in touch. Ndu, Cameroon, is fairly remote. For many months they had no Internet available, so they wrote me letters and mailed them by snail mail. It took two months for their letters to reach me, and if I responded, it took weeks and weeks for them to get my reply. In another era not so long ago, this is how it was if you had loved ones separated by distance, especially overseas. It is a very limiting factor to loving your microcommunity.

If you want to regularly express your love to your microcommunity in the twenty-first century, you must learn to use the technology available today. My children feel loved when I post something onto their Facebook walls. They also feel slighted if I ignore their texts. Birthdays, Valentine's Day, and daily compliments and care are all made richer in expressing love when utilizing the opportunities of technology. I had to decide that I love my microcommunity more than I dislike the learning curve of using the technology. This is not meant to suggest that physically spending time with each other doesn't generate great power. What great power shoots through us in a hug, a visible smile (instead of an emoticon), and just through the pleasure of sitting close to each other and sharing conversation over chai, coffee, or a meal. However, when that is not possible because of the global reality of our culture, then wholehearted people learn to love their microcommunity in every way available to them, utilizing technology to supplement the richness of relationships that are given to us by God as a gift of His blessing. Wholehearted church planters are learning this in the reality of a global microcommunity.

Loving Your Team and Friends

Wholehearted church planters have a passion for the people with whom they are partners in ministry and friendships. Some of the most loyal friends I have are the people who are team members. In the church planting context, few things are more important than expressing the value of other team members to the Kingdom of God. Just like in a marriage, people need to be affirmed, and need to feel important to the team.

If a church plant is perceived through the eyes of business efficiency, then people on the church planting team are viewed as human resources. Their value is measured by performance of a task and/or how it affects the bottom line. In business, the bottom line is profit. In church planting in the business model, the bottom line is the way we measure success: "nickels and noses"—that is, money and head count.

We can argue for much more biblical ways to plant churches than the organizational business model. If we view the church as a living organism (different than an organization), such as the bride of Christ or the body of Christ, then people of the team are valuable for much different reasons. John 3:16 reminds us that God loved all the people in the world so much that He sent His Son to be our Savior. Being like Jesus means we value people because God values people, not because of what they do but just because of who they are already.

Through the years I have served at different churches and have had teams at each place. I have made many mistakes in showing value to my teammates, but I have learned and am still learning to love the people who are my teammates. In the current church I am in, we celebrated our tenth anniversary last year (2012). Because of the nature of a network, my team has changed through several seasons of the church. We are starting several churches every year, we are doing missions in many contexts simultaneously, and, in actuality, I have several teams that I am a part of on a weekly basis.

I consider my family to be a team, as we use our home and family resources to minister together to many different people we love. I consider the local church where I serve to be a team, as we worship together, encourage each other, sponsor church plants, work on local community transformation projects, and even travel together on mission trips. I consider the network leaders to be a team as we plant new churches together, partner together in missions, encourage one another, and pray for each other. I consider our nonprofit, Ethne Global Services, to be a team as we cooperate, dream, resource, work together, and celebrate victories in helping people. I consider the seminary faculty and staff a team, as we work together to creatively educate new leaders in the Kingdom of God. In any given week, I work in all these contexts of team, and any one person in my life might be on several different "teams." My wife is in my life as family, church, and network. Kenny Moore is in my life in the context of church, network, and Ethne Global Services, the nonprofit. Many people are my teammates in more than one context. We need to be better at loving our teammates in the same way that we show love to the people/place to whom and where God has called us to serve.

Practical Ways to Love Your Team and Friends

Many "languages of love" communicate your love to your team and friends. Gary Chapman introduced to us to the five classic languages in his bestseller, *The Five Love Languages*. These languages are "words of affirmation," "quality time," "receiving gifts," "acts of service," and "physical touch."[2] Other cultures show love by giving hospitality, sharing food, and an openness to include a person in their literal family relationships.

Sometimes the best way to love is to pray for people and for them to know they are being prayed for, perhaps even in their presence. The key element here is that when you love someone, you learn to be thoughtful and to consider how that person needs to experience the genuine messages that you care for that person. I am embarrassed that I seem to be such a slow learner in this area of my life, but at least I understand how important it is to relational health.

Here are some suggestions of things I am learning in how to relate to others:

1. be considerate in giving credit;
2. be generous in giving thanks and appreciation;
3. be sincere in compliments;
4. deflect attention to others;
5. be generous with opportunities;
6. invite others along anywhere you go if possible;
7. be creative in maximizing the giftedness of others;
8. listen and learn from your family, team, and friends;
9. pray without ceasing for your microcommunity.

Summary

Wholehearted church planters have rich microcommunities, often several overlapping layers of them. Wholehearted church planters are rich in relationships. They are constantly learning new ways to love the various relationships of people in their microcommunities. They are creative and thoughtful in expressing their love because it is a priority for them. They are learning to be greathearted as they love and are loved by God. They intentionally show His love to others in their microcommunities as the Holy Spirit empowers them.

Chapter 11

Loving a People

ALLAN KARR

We can do no great things—only small things with great love. –MOTHER
TERESA

Falling in Love with a People

In 2009, I visited the jungle refugee camp on the border of Burma and
Thailand where my adopted children are from, Mae La Camp.[1] It was a
relatively small area jam-packed with over 70,000 refugees who had been
displaced by the longest civil war in the world. The Karen tribe is a mi-
nority tribe in Burma. They had been targeted for ethnic extermination
since at least the 1960s. Hundreds of thousands of Karen people had been
shelled and burned out of their native villages and homeland, and were
in tragic transition.

The refugee camp was a temporary place of security, yet for many
it was still like a prison. Many refugees had lived there for over twenty
years. I lived in my mentor's home, Dr. Simon, with many orphans who
had lost their parents in the conflict. Some of the children were "orphans"
who had been separated under adverse circumstances from a parent. I
heard their stories of pain and suffering. I visited the home where the
men who had been handicapped by land mines were living daily with the
reminders of the crimes committed against them and their tribal people:
their limbs and eyes were destroyed and missing. I listened to Dr. Simon
teach me the tragic history of his people and the region and watched him
respond with the fruits of the Spirit: love, joy, peace, patience, kindness,
goodness, faithfulness, gentleness, and self-control.[2] In April 2012, the entire seminary compound, the orphanage, and Dr. Simon's home were re-
duced to ashes by a fire, a complete loss. Simon returned from a wedding
to see the loss. After a few minutes he called a time of worship to praise
God, in spite of the circumstances. I continually marvel at the resilience of
the Karen people, who remain friendly and smiling to outsiders like me,
even including me as family, in spite of all their experiences.

In the beginning of my journey with the Karen I was sometimes angry. My sense of justice was offended to the maximum, and I wanted to somehow retaliate against the evil forces of government that caused all of this pain and suffering. Then I realized that my impulse to take up arms and trudge into the jungle was emotional folly. Besides being past my prime physically and untrained, I knew physical retaliation was not the response God was directing me towards. I knew if I was going to fight for justice, my strongest weapons were my mouth and my brain, in the power of the Holy Spirit. However, unexpected fruit grew deep inside me. I fell deeply in love with this people group. It caught me unexpectedly. They aren't like me culturally. We don't share all the same values. They sometimes are ethnocentric in a way that offends me. At times I get irritated with their shortsightedness. However, I realized that despite the differences, I still love them deeply.

Loving People with the Resources of My Life

I decided that the best way to help my refugee friends is to educate and to organize. "Education" is expressed on two fronts: the refugees and the rest of the world. Education in the refugee context means setting up schools and teaching in existing schools. Educating the rest of the world involves bringing to light this conflict that has been largely invisible to global awareness for far too long. "Organization" means setting up a nonprofit[3] that helps refugees in the United States assimilate holistically into their new communities, and which partners overseas to transform humanitarian community by creating orphanages, preventing human trafficking, etc. This effort is now bearing much fruit, but the fruit comes only as a missionary loves a people and that love becomes contagious to others.

As a younger man, I always marveled when I heard some missionaries speak about their people, their tribe, and their place where they were called. I could sense a great passion that they had. They made it quite clear that they were called to be exactly where they were for that season of their lives. Over family gatherings, I have listened to my wife's brother and sister-in-law, Mel and Nancy Skinner, talk about their ministry in Russia and to different Russian people groups for over twenty years. They love their people, and they love their place. They have invested their lives loving these people in word and deed for the bulk of their adult lives. Many of my friends through the years have spoken with equal passion about their people and places. I think something deep within God's people makes us want to connect to the work to which God has called us so that we live with this kind of commitment and love.

In 1995, God called my family to Castle Rock, Colorado, to plant a church. At the time, coaches helped make decisions like that by finding where doors were open and where great need or potential existed. We were encouraged to get alignment of all the logistics, such as partnerships and funding. We visited Castle Rock for a few hours before we made our decision to move our family across the country and start a new life in this "parachute drop" church planting effort. Very soon after we moved to Castle Rock, we fell in love with the culture of the place. After a while, we fell in love with a growing group of our community, where we experienced communitas in the church planting efforts. We later recognized we loved the people and the place and articulated a deep sense of calling to both.

While it works out for many people, this was sort of an "old school" way of church planting. In retrospect, I learned from that experience. Now I teach my students to follow a more "inside out" approach[4] to deciding where God is calling them to plant and invest their lives. Often my phone rings. A potential planter is calling to inquire about planting a church in my state or my area. They ask many of the same questions I asked decades ago about funding, logistics, and potential. I understand their questions, but I ask questions that frustrate the business values of the way many of us were taught to pursue this endeavor. The truth is, I have rarely seen a place where we don't need more churches. I haven't found a place without need for Christian witness and community. If "need" is the primary criteria, we need new churches everywhere.

I often ask a question, "Do you love the people and the community you are asking me about?" Often they are like I was, never having had the opportunity to even live or know the place they are asking about. I now encourage potential missionary church planters to pray that God will give them a wholehearted love for a people in whom they would devote their time and energy. I think you can love people without having met them, but I still think that you should be able to be articulate that love.

Ups and Downs

Church planters who love their people and their places approach the mission differently. They survive the ups and downs, the discouragements and challenges, because they have a deeper sense of calling. The calling is a love for the people of their mission, an ingredient and symptom of being wholehearted church planters.

The chart on page 85 shows the simulated ups and downs in the life of pastoring an existing established church in traditional ministry and in planting a new church. Traditional ministry has ups and downs in stress and emotional energy. Church planting has ups and downs as well. However, in church planting the highs are generally higher and the lows tend to be lower. Sometimes, even in the same day, a planter will experience a peak in the morning and a valley in the afternoon, or vice versa. Literally, you could be totally stressed in the morning, and then something great happens and the day totally changes moods. During the inevitable valleys, church planters are tempted to throw in the towel. One of the strongest preventions to quitting and to being able to be resilient in the face of discouragement is a deep sense of calling that comes from the deep sense

Church Planting Ups and Downs

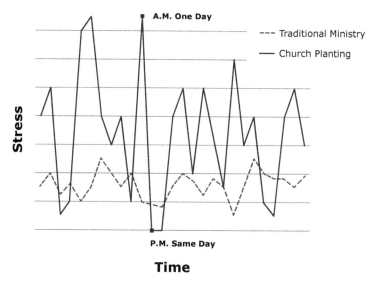

A.M. One Day

--- Traditional Ministry

— Church Planting

Stress

P.M. Same Day

Time

of love for a people and a place where God has sent you. When my wife Kathy speaks about her calling, she says, "I found church planting to be very exciting but also very hard, time-consuming work for my family and me. I really pray that each of you has a strong sense of call for what you are about to be a part of in church planting. If you get to a point where you are struggling or seem to hit a wall, it is very important to be able to fall back on your calling."[5] This calling includes obedience to God, but is built on a platform of loving the people and place where God asks you to serve. This is an important aspect of being wholehearted.

Loving a People Means Respecting and Caring

"Loving a people" means learning how to respect and care about the communities where they live, work, and play. I have been the lead planter for two churches. In my first church plant, I learned to respect and care for my community of Castle Rock and the people who lived there. My love for the people grew to the point that I loved the people more than I loved the idea of the church plant. Let me explain. In my community we ended up planting two *additional* new churches because we loved the people of our community. In one case, we discovered a significant part of our community was "cowboy culture," perhaps as much as 40 percent of the population if you include the indigenous families who settled the area up to a century before. However, none of the people of that culture were coming to our attractional services. We ended up calling a cowboy church planter to the area. God opened doors, began reaching out to that part of the culture, and eventually planted a new church. Some couldn't understand why we would decide to plant a new church when our church plant was still fledgling. It was because we ultimately loved the people more than we loved the image of our church plant being successful. Besides, planting a new church was "successful" in the Kingdom, even if some people did not see it as such at the time.

In the second case, we discovered an entire apartment complex in Castle Rock where approximately 5000 people lived, a population greater than that of many Colorado towns. No one from that complex was part of our church. Ultimately, as we started to pray, God opened the door to start a new mission church in that complex. It eventually evolved into a Spanish language church, and for the lifespan of the church it met within the apartment complex, sometimes meeting in a tenant's apartment and sometimes in one of the clubhouses. The need for the new church became evident when we realized that in spite of our best efforts and hopes, the great majority of people of that complex were not responsive to invitations to be part of the sponsoring church plant where I was lead pastor. Out of a wholehearted respect and care for that community of people, we decided it was better to plant the new church.

When wholehearted people love other people, they respect and care for their community. I never gave consideration to care about the Colfax corridor of Denver and Aurora, Colorado, until it became the primary residential area of the Karen refugees. In spite of its crime and economically depressed conditions, we started to care for this area of the Denver metro. Why? It is where people that we love lived. I never would have known I would spend so much energy and time in that part of the metropolitan area until God revealed a love I had for the Karen refugees He had brought to our city. This is where they lived, so it only followed that we would start caring for their community.

Loving a People Means Understanding Their Needs

When you begin to understand the needs of people whom you love, it sometimes changes your opinions on issues you thought you were convinced about. In the late 1990s we completed an assessment of the needs of our community in Castle Rock. Through interviews with leaders and others in the community we discovered many needs to which we were previously blind. For example, we learned from the police that a major crime issue in our community was domestic violence and that the area had no place of refuge for abused women. Our church donated towards and helped organize a home set up for law enforcement officers to have a place to take women in precarious situations. We learned that, in spite of all the nice neighborhoods that appeared idyllic, debt, bankruptcy, and financial crisis were destroying families. We decided that classes on financial management in conjunction with biblical principles were a key need in the community. We did not think this was necessarily a "church planting" activity, but discovered along the way that when you understand the needs of people you love, you change your ideas and direction of your energies. Such changes became part of our church planting strategy.

Furthermore, I have historically tended to be very conservative in my view of social programs from the government. I believed that many abuses of social programs were destructive to the overall health of our nation. I still believe this to be true. However, after 2007, in seeing the struggles the refugees whom I love had assimilating into our culture, my heart softened. I found myself wishing that more of the social program budget of our government could find its way productively into helping the refugees that we love.

One example focuses on the atrocities of the dental needs of the adult refugees. They could not afford dental care in any way, and our social programs made no provision for this. Our church worked hard for about a year getting people to dentists who donated their services or discounted their fees. Then we paid the fees as needed. What we did was just a drop in the bucket of meeting the needs. I looked at the way funds from social programs were spent or not spent and longed for reform. Republicans were hesitant to increase the social program budget, and Democrats wanted to spend the money in ways with which I often disagreed. No agreeable, equitable solution has been reached on this issue, so that basically the same situation faces us today. This whole issue developed because we saw the needs of the people we loved. Wholehearted planters see the needs of their community and give attention, energy, and resources towards meeting those needs.

Loving a People Includes Mourning

"Loving a people" means that because of your love you empathize with your people. You learn how to mourn when that community mourns. At first it is a learning experience, but it eventually becomes innate. I previously mentioned that, in April 2012, a giant fire destroyed my friend Dr. Simon's home in Mae La Camp in Thailand along with the seminary compound, the orphanage, and the staff and visitors dorms. I received word almost immediately and then a few hours later watched the video footage posted on-line. I have read in novels that when people fight to avoid crying, sometimes their eyes burn. For the first time in my life that I remember, my eyes burned. Later, I stopped fighting it and just cried. I was grieving deeply for the loss experienced by people whom I love. I was grieving with my whole heart.

In the summer of 2011, I was in Burma and went to visit a village of my friend Saw Yaha Lay Lay La. He is the pastor in that village. A woman there had recently died. I went to the home where the body lay in the main room and where the family had been congregated in mourning for several days. They were all grieving deeply. I found myself genuinely mourning as well for a person I had never met. Upon reflection, I realized that when people I love grieve, my love for them moves me to mourn as well. This is how wholehearted people respond when the community that they love is mourning.

Mourning with your people will likely look different in each context. People mourn when they experience loss, and loss comes in a variety of contexts. Fans of sport teams mourn losses. People mourn political losses. We mourn losses from natural disasters. We mourn loss of employment and missed opportunities. We mourn broken relationships and conflict. If you are not native to the people and community that you love, you will know you truly love them when you start mourning the sense of loss they mourn. This sign of loving your people is characteristic of being wholehearted. Mourning when they are mourning is loving your neighbor as yourself.

Loving a People Means Celebrating

The other side of the coin from mourning is celebration. "Loving a people" includes rejoicing in the things that bring them pride, happiness, and satisfaction. Most of us have grown up in our own culture conditioned to know what is worth celebrating. In the United States, many people are emotionally tied to a college sports team–often from American football, a game really appreciated only in the United States. The rest of the world doesn't know about or care about which team wins the college football bowl game that decides the national championship. Conversely, the rest of the world is very focused on the World Cup for *futbol* (what Americans call "soccer"). While it has gradually started changing, most Americans still aren't even aware of World Cup competition days or which teams are playing.

When my family lived in Madrid, Spain, in the summer of 2006, the World Cup was going on. When the Spanish national team was playing, the streets were deserted, because everyone was watching it on TV. (It was being played in Germany.) When Spain scored a goal, the city erupted in celebration, complete with fireworks. We could hear the city celebrating through the open window of our balcony. The first week, we didn't get it. After a while, we found our family scheduling our time to ensure we could watch the games. We even joined the loud cheering when Spain scored a goal. It was important to people we cared about, so it became important to us.

Wholehearted church planters learn what is important to the people God has called us to love. We intuitively know not to belittle or make fun of those things important to our people. To the contrary, because we love the people, those things important to the people we love become important to us too.

Many people have moved to be planters in cultures where they are outsiders to the culture. Instead of embracing and loving the new culture, they have resisted, belittled, and refused to embrace the things that are very important to the people that were the focus of the new church planting effort. Planting efforts like this are normally short-lived. The planters are exposed in the sense that it becomes clear that they love the idea of church planting more than the love the people of that community. When you love the people, you celebrate genuinely what they celebrate. This love grows in the heart as a genuine expression of the love for this people.

Loving a People Includes Hospitality

Wholehearted church planters tend to be very hospitable. My co-author Linda and her family have opened their home to thousands of people through the years. This process of genuine hospitality is common for wholehearted church planters. Our family has historically been very hospitable. My wife has been very patient with my on-the-spot invitations. She has a big, generous heart and so constantly shares our home and life with others. Loving a people means practicing hospitality among our community and microcommunity.

Staying throughout the world in the homes of people in villages with no electricity, plumbing, or even beds may not always be the most comfortable situation, but I have discovered it is the direct route to intimacy with the hearts of people. I recently stayed in the small village home of my brother in Christ, Yesupadam Kommuri, in Andra Pradesh, India. We were already extremely close, but my team's willingness to stay in their small two-room home (with no toilet and no running water) grew an intimacy that cannot be duplicated or even understood. We just love each other more deeply. We were humbled that they would proudly sacrifice to share their home with us. They were honored we were willing to stay with them. The result was greater intimacy among friends.

We have hosted hundreds or thousands of people in our home throughout the years. Our hospitality comes very naturally to us and opens many doors for closer relationships that have benefited the Kingdom of God. All over the world, wholehearted people intuitively understand that hospitality is a characteristic of godly people. This elementary principle is true and effective for people God has called to be church planters. Putting the principal to practice often comes so naturally that church planters don't see it as anything other than normal.

Loving a People Includes Loving Strangers

In John 14:15, Jesus said, "If you love Me, you will keep My commandments" (NASB). One of those commandments is given after Jesus taught the parable of the "Good Samaritan" in Luke 10. Jesus was using the story to answer the question asked of Him, "And who is my neighbor?" (Lk. 10:29). Jesus told the story about a man who helped a stranger/enemy along the roadside. After telling the now well-known parable, Jesus asked who best demonstrated neighborliness towards the man in need. The answer was not the religious leaders who passed him by but the unnamed enemy/stranger we now call the "Good Samaritan." Jesus then gave a command, "Go and do the same" (Lk. 10:37, NASB). To follow this command, we have to leave the gathering of believers wherever they meet and live out our faith in the everyday circumstances of life. "Loving a people" means extending hospitality to newcomers and strangers. This is possible in almost every community in the world.

In 2012, I was teaching a class in Phoenix, Arizona. One of my friends whose wedding ceremony I had performed, Kay Kay, was a refugee who had recently moved to the city from Denver. I asked her to speak in my class. At the end of her excellent presentation people asked questions.

One student asked, "What has surprised you the most since moving to America?"

Her answer shocked most in the class. She said she was shocked a nation of prosperity had so many homeless people. She stated, "Even in the villages in the jungle or refugee camps where we had nothing, there were no homeless people. We would never let someone sleep under a bridge when it was cold outside."

She admitted that it was heartbreaking to her. Several times when she had virtually no money, she felt compelled to buy homeless people some food. The issues of homelessness in America are complex, and Kay Kay may be naïve to some of that complexity; yet to her the solution to the problem was relatively simple. Jesus told us to love our neighbor, and then illustrated this with a story about a stranger helping his enemy in a potentially dangerous circumstance. Then Jesus told us to go and live that way. Wholehearted people, and especially wholehearted church planters, live out this command. God has made us keenly aware of the need for Christians to be aware of how we can appropriately show the love of God to strangers. I do not give money directly to homeless people because of the long history of the needy using it for bad life decisions. However, I will regularly buy hungry people a meal. We use church offerings for assisting homeless in getting into homes through an initiative in our city. We donate our furniture and clothes and our time to move people into housing. We give to the needs of refugees. We feel responsible for widows and orphans (Jas. 1:27). We hope that disciples from our church dispel the impression that Christians do not care for others. We want to live out the commands of Christ, up to and especially including showing love to strangers in our community. Wholehearted church planters live this way even if the people they serve will never be a part of the church plant.

Wholehearted church planters love people. They love people in general, and they specifically love the people whom God has called them to serve. As they express their love to people, they do not just find ways to check some activities off the list. Instead, they show evidence of a love that has holistically taken root in the heart of the church-planting missionary and becomes contagious as she lives life and makes disciples. It is seen as a genuine expression of his love of the people to whom he is called to serve and share the gospel.

Chapter 12

Discovering Your Missional Love Language

LINDA BERGQUIST

Love is a verb. –GARY CHAPMAN, AUTHOR OF *THE FIVE LOVE LANGUAGES*

Many years ago, New York Times' best-selling author Gary Chapman coined a now-familiar way of thinking about how people give and receive love. He wrote about five universal love languages and about how learning those languages can help people understand, bless, and relate to one another better.[1] He describes the love languages as "words of affirmation," "quality time," "receiving gifts," "acts of service," and "physical touch." Based on Chapman's paradigm, this chapter suggests five similar dimensions of a *missional* love language. The idea of love languages as used in this chapter implies a desire to form wholehearted, yet intentionally missional, church planting relationships between church planters and their partners, church planters and their teams, and church planters and their communities. Remember our criteria that church planters must know and love people.

Love Language #1: Words of Affirmation

Partnering Churches Honor Their Daughter Churches

Mentors and supporting congregations best affirm their church planters by believing in them. Planters need loyal *friends* who will hope, imagine, and dream with them. They need enthusiastic *fans* to publicly cheer them on, and they need *family* members who will come around the baby church and love it enough to believe in its future. Sometimes churches call the churches they start *daughter* churches. This implies a close relationship, even a familial bond. Church planters also need blessing from spiritual "fathers" and "mothers" who mentor them or play other significant roles in their lives. Of His own Son, God said, "This is my Son, whom I love; with him I am well pleased" (Mt. 3:17). Those who come around church planters can strengthen their spirits by writing encouraging notes, bragging on them publicly, letting them know that they are pleasing to them. They can affirm, empower, guide, forgive, thank, and commend them with sincere, heartfelt words. Sometimes, tough love is needed. In those times, those who have given real affirmation are best able to navigate the truth/grace intersection. Proverbs offers this: "Better is open rebuke / than hidden love. / Wounds from a friend can be trusted, / but an enemy multiplies kisses" (Prov. 27:5–6).

Church Planters Encourage Their Teams

Most church planters work hard, putting in long hours. They look for team members who are hard workers, too. They are grateful for the help, but sometimes they are so task-driven that they forget that their teams need to be acknowledged. Church planters, please encourage others in their gifts and talents! Remind them how valuable they are, not just because of their work, but because of who they are. Bless them even when they fail. Say thank you often. It never gets old. Say we a lot and I seldom when you celebrate what God is doing through the new church.

Church Planters Affirm Their Communities

Scott and Julie Berglin are long-time residents of Pleasanton, California, where they are starting Rock Bible Church. Besides starting a church, Scott is a volunteer soccer coach and Julie is a public school teacher. The Berglins' love for their town is evident. They quite naturally speak positively about Pleasanton, and they pray for it because they cared about it long before they started a church there. Another Scott in a different North American town moved there because it was a quickly growing new suburb where he imagined planting a great church. He refers to it as his "target community." There is nothing really wrong with that, but can you see the difference? When this second Scott dreams about his vision, it is faceless and nameless. He will need to work much harder to gain the trust of his new community and to learn to love his adopted home with all of his heart in the way that Scott and Julie Berglin already do.

Many years ago, Linda's friend Evan ran in San Francisco's infamous "Bay to Breakers" race. Many runners dress in costume for the race, and, that day, Evan dressed as a Catholic religious leader. As he ran, people watching from the sidelines thrust their children into his arms to receive blessing. People seemed so hungry for blessing that even a fake religious leader seemed good enough. Some San Franciscan parishes host events to bless animals, to which scores of people bring their pets. In what ways can you as a church planter pronounce blessing on your community?

Love Language #2: Quality Time

Re-gifting the Gift of Time

Author Dorothy Bass asks, "How might our experience of time change if we could learn to receive time as a gift of God?"[2] Time is a gift from God, and some of that time is intended to be "re-gifted" by being given back to others. At a gathering of leaders sent out by Hope Church in Fort Worth, Texas, one person made an incredible announcement, "I don't think that any of my conversations with Harold Bullock (his mentor and Hope's founding pastor) have ever been ended by him. He always lets me be the one to tell him when our conversation was over." Harold is a busy man, but he takes mentoring seriously. The track record of individuals and families whom he has influenced and who are now serving God all over the world is evidence of his time commitment to others.

In the mid-1980s, Doyle Braden, a regional missions director in Southern California, invited Linda and her friend to help survey a Cambodian refugee community in Long Beach, California. Braden walked neighborhoods and knocked on doors all day long with the rookie team. His time investment was so unusual and so unanticipated that Linda recognized and remembered Braden's gift of himself. Spending time with planters is one of the most effective ways by which mentors can transmit wholehearted DNA from mentor to planter. If distance is a problem, try a Skype call from a computer with a camera. Take a planter, or a whole church planting team, to breakfast, coffee, or even home for dinner. Visit their churches, especially the first service of a new church.

The Meaning of Time Across Cultures

As a new Christian, Linda visited a church with a ministry to Southeast Asian refugees. She waited with a stalwart leader from the host congregation for the ministry bus to arrive so the church service could begin. When the bus was fifteen minutes late, the man muttered in exasperation, "Where are they? Everyone knows that God is prompt!" The leader's comment displayed his apparent motto: Love is not patient. A few years later when Linda needed to cement a relationship with another group of Southeast Asians in a different city, she was invited to sleep overnight at a family's home. That night everyone slept on the floor on mats, and, the next morning, they sent their teenage daughter to live with Linda's family to help start a church fifteen hundred miles away. Quality time translated, "Be present. Give the gift of time by spending the night with our family." Time means different things in different cultures, and wholehearted church planters are people who care enough to try to interpret time through the worldview lenses of others.

Giving Quality Time to a Community

When the San Francisco Giants won the World Series in 2010, Linda and her husband, fair weather fans of the team, attended the city's outdoor broadcast of the final game. They were also present for the citywide ticker-tape parade. It was about rejoicing with those who rejoice, another way of loving a community and giving time away wisely. Sometimes you have to weep with a city. When San Francisco finds reason to mourn, rejoice, or protest, it moves into the streets to be together. For the events of the

1934 General Strike, various war protests, or the 1978 slaying of its mayor, thousands of San Franciscans gathered at the Ferry Building and marched down Market Street to the plaza in front of their city hall. Other cities turn out for Fourth of July parades, fairs, festivals, and fireworks. Whatever ignites the passion of a particular place should also capture the hearts of church planters who love the people of their towns and cities. Learning about people and becoming involved with them shows the city they care enough to give their time.

Love Language #3: Receiving Gifts

Gifts That Help New Churches and Gifts That Hinder Them

When thinking about what support systems a church planter needs from a partner or sending church, the first thing that comes to most people's minds is financial support. Certainly most kinds of new churches need some money. Money is used for salaries and benefits, supplies, Bibles, rentals, and more, depending on the new church's paradigm. However, some kinds of new churches–for instance, house church networks–may be hindered by outside support because paying indigenous leaders hampers their capacity for rapid reproduction. No matter what the gift, it is important for the church planter to value both gift and giver and to understand gift giving relationally. Thank-you notes, accountability measures, and handling funds respectfully are indicators of grateful hearts. Church planters welcome other practical expressions of giving. These include things such as gift cards to coffee shops, family memberships to zoos and museums (especially for newcomers in town), new or used computers and audiovisual equipment, office space in a church building, or hosting new church "baby showers."[3]

Church Planters Give Back

Both giving and receiving are built into the Christian tradition: "For God so loved the world, that He gave..." (Jn. 3:16, NASB). Just as church planters receive from others, they are responsible for giving back. One way planters bless their teams is by sharing resources with them, including the funds they personally raise to plant their churches. Some churches keep salaries equitable among all team members. Sometimes new churches offer free books or Bibles to newcomers. Other new congregations take muffins or cookies to visitors. Some churches choose to give the entire offering from their launch services back to their communities as first fruits of their commitment to give back. Be aware, however, that while communities support generous congregations, nobody is impressed by churches that brag about their generosity.

Love Language #4: Acts of Service

Another way to invest in a new church plant is to serve it. Gary Irby, a Seattle-based church planting strategist, coined the phrase "pray, pay, and play" to describe ways to get involved with church starts. The first two are easy to interpret, but the third is less familiar. By *play*, Irby is referring to direct, on-the-ground pairing of partnering and sending congregations with new churches. This can include sending core group members for the church plant, but it can also mean that the entire sending congregation gets involved through providing teams to help with evangelistic projects, new church preview services, survey work, distributing door hangers, assisting with community activities and events, painting a house or a school where a new church meets, or serving in any of a myriad of ways. Serving is one of the best ways to transfer wholehearted DNA to potential leaders.

Serving as a Way of Life

At a train station in Rajasthan, India, a man with a red turban asked Linda's husband, Eric, if he could shine his tennis shoes. The idea was not very practical, but Eric could see that the man needed work, so he asked him to shine the shoes of the man near him, a baggage carrier. When the shoe shiner knelt on the ground, Eric joined him there. Within a few minutes a crowd had gathered behind the three men to watch what seemed to be an unheard-of event—an American tourist kneeling beside lower cast Indian men. Completely unaware, Eric conversed with the two men while the shoes became shiny. The scene was a reminder of Jesus washing His disciples' feet. Jesus "knew that the Father had put all things under his power, and that he had come from God and was returning to God" (Jn. 13:3), but what did He decide to do with all of His authority? He chose to serve. "He got up from the meal, took off his outer clothing, and wrapped a towel around his waist" (13:4). The only way to teach wholehearted servant leadership is by practicing it joyfully as a way of life. Partner church pastors who serve church planters and church planters who serve their teams are good role models and DNA code bearers for next-generation leaders.

New Churches Serving Their Communities

Just weeks after arriving in San Jose, California, with his team, church planter Andy Wood approached his new city to offer the service of his team to help the city set up for and clean up from their annual arts festival. They asked nothing in return, but rallied partner churches and their own small team as city helpers. At the end of the event, the city event planners thanked the yet unformed church with tears in their eyes and invited their involvement in all citywide activities.

Glenn Woodward, who planted Generation City in San Diego County, intentionally lives at poverty level, even growing his own vegetables just to make ends meet, thus identifying with his larger community. The church assists the homeless, helps people find jobs, and sponsors community cleanup days on which they pick up trash and paint over unsightly graffiti. Also in San Diego County, Victor Schloss is starting a church among artists and musicians. The church volunteers in its community by directing traffic at arts events and helping to set up block parties where local musicians perform. Other San Diego church plants do "extreme makeovers" of elementary schools. They paint classrooms, invest in landscaping, and stripe parking lots, quietly serving in the name of Jesus.

Love Language #5: Meaningful Touch

In incorporating the concepts of his love languages into this book, Linda and Allan have stayed true to the meaning as intended by Gary Chapman in most cases. However, we decided that in the category of *Meaningful Touch*, we would discuss both *Physical Touch* and *Spiritual Touch*–namely, prayer. Certainly physical touch is important in every relationship, but prayer is such a dense expression of missional relationship that it cannot be tucked neatly into another category.

Physical Touch

By expanding the concept of touch for the purposes of this book, we do not want to undermine the importance of physical touch one iota. It is good and appropriate for Christian communities to learn how to hug, to offer a "holy kiss" (Rom. 16:16), and to show affection in other appropriate ways. Christians should be able to comfort hurting or lonely people, widows and widowers, military spouses, and simply people for whom physical touch is an important expression of friendship. That handshake at the church door, the time of greeting or the passing of the peace in worship services, or the fact that someone sits next to them at a church event is an indicator of a friendly and loving church for others.

God also uses physical touch, or the practice of the laying on of hands, for extending blessing, commissioning, and healing. Isaac blessed his son, Jacob, this way (Gen. 27:27), and people brought their children to be blessed by Jesus' hands (Mt. 9:13–15). Again, in the Old Testament, "Aaron lifted up his hands toward the people and blessed them..." (Lev. 9:22, NASB). At the end of worship services, many pastors bless their congregations as they extend their hands towards them in like manner.

Physical touch is also used in the ministry of healing. Jairus, a synagogue leader, begged Jesus to come to his home and put His hands on his dying daughter so that she would live (Mk. 5:22–23). The Lord touched the eyes of two blind men, and by faith, they could see (Mt. 9:28–31). Scripture says that after He rebuked the fever that had overtaken Simon's mother, many people came to Jesus for healing. He laid hands on each one, and they were healed from physical ailments and from demons. Healing stories abound not only in the New Testament, but also in testimonies of people all over the world today. Through healing is one way that people come to know who God is and to put their trust in Christ. Revivals, church planting movements, and other occurrences that can only be explained by the presence of God frequently include healing phenomena.

Finally, Scripture also supports the laying on of hands for commission-ing, for spiritual gifts or enduring spiritual gifts, and for power on future leaders. Moses laid hands on Joshua, who would succeed him, and Joshua was "filled with the Spirit of wisdom" (Deut. 34:9). This practice continued through the generations and into the early church. When the church in Jerusalem was brand new, leaders were chosen to support the apostles in practical ministries. After they selected these leaders, they brought them to the apostles, who prayed and laid hands on them. The Spirit told the Antioch church to separate Barnabas and Saul for a particular ministry. In response, the church laid hands on the men and sent them out (Acts 13:1–3). Laying on of hands for ministry was apparently an unusual event, but it was still one to be taken quite seriously. First Timothy 5:22 says, "Do not be hasty in the laying on of hands..." The formal enduing of power is perhaps a potential missionary practice that can remind missionary-type church planters and sending churches that they need to reproduce leadership.

Spiritual Touch Through Prayer

Imagine the apostle Paul's beautiful prayer for the Christians of Ephesus:

> For this reason I kneel before the Father, from whom every fam-ily in heaven and on earth derives its name. I pray that out of his glorious riches he may strengthen you with power through his Spirit in your inner being, so that Christ may dwell in your hearts through faith. And I pray that you, being rooted and established in love, may have power, together with all the Lord's holy people, to grasp how wide and long and high and deep is the love of Christ, and to know this love that surpasses knowledge–that you may be filled to the measure of all the fullness of God. (Eph.3:14–19)

The love of Paul, a church-planting missionary, for God's church is appar-ent in these verses. He is not only concerned that the Ephesians maintain purity or reproduce disciples. He also wants them to know and be filled with the love of God. As Paul traveled on many missionary journeys, his touch was never far away from the churches he started because he prayed for them and wrote them letters. The churches reciprocated, sending mes-sengers, laborers, and gifts to the apostle. While Paul deeply loved the churches he started, nevertheless, he kept moving to places where the message of the Kingdom had not yet been heard.

How Church Planters Touch Their Communities Through Prayer

Reggie McNeal wrote, "Prayer may be the most untapped and underused resource available to the church for accomplishing its mission."[4] Linda and Allan agree. We have shared our practice of Luke 10:2 prayer in so many circles that we have lost count of how many people set alarms for 10:02 each morning, praying that the Lord of the Harvest will send laborers to our fields. When we hear other alarms vibrating around us, we observe knowing looks–"So you are a part of this prayer fellowship too!"

Recently, two shifts to this practice of prayer have been initiated in the church planting community. First, instead of praying just for new church planters, people are beginning to pray that God will raise up laborers who represent the five-fold gifts in Ephesians 4:11–13–apostles, prophets, evangelists, pastors, and teachers. It grieves us that for so long we have been asking according to our own job designations rather than the Father's. The second shift is adding a second prayer time each day. At 7:14 p.m., the second time the clock turns that time each day, Christians are stopping to pray 2 Chronicles 7:14 for themselves and for their communities: "If my people, who are called by my name, will humble themselves and pray and seek my face and turn from their wicked ways, then I will hear from heaven, and I will forgive their sin and will heal their land" (2 Chr. 7:14).

Since wholehearted church planters are people who are learning to love God with all of their hearts, souls, strength, and minds, it follows that they are also learning what it means to abide in Christ. Jesus said, "If you remain in me and my words remain in you, ask whatever you wish, and it will be done for you" (Jn. 15:7). Those who abide in Christ can have assurance that God hears their prayers. They pray for the spiritual well being of their communities, for their neighbors who mourn, for families, for the futures of the children living in them. They pray for their neighborhood while jogging its streets or walking their dogs: "I urge, then, first of all, that petitions, prayers, intercession and thanksgiving be made for all people–for kings and all those in authority, that we may live peaceful and quiet lives in all godliness and holiness. This is good, and pleases God our Savior, who wants all people to be saved and to come to a knowledge of the truth" (1 Tim. 2:1–4).

Linda remembers an experience while she lived and worked as a church planter in San Diego. She felt impressed to stop and pray at some particular empty city lots. A church building now stands in each of those places. Church planters, pray as if you were pastoring a whole community and not just members and attendees of the church you started. Pray for the success of other nearby churches. Pray for the connections that people in your community have to the rest of the world, and pray that God's Kingdom comes in your city, town, or neighborhood.

In his classic book, *The Meaning of Prayer*, Harry Emerson Fosdick addressed a concept he called *prayer as dominant desire*. He saw prayer as an indomitable force of human existence, believing that prayer is "the inward measure if any man's quality."[5] This kind of prayer consumes a person's whole being. One cannot release it because it simply *must* come to be. It is a wholehearted exercise of body, mind, and soul, perhaps much like James's fervent, effectual prayer of a righteous person (Jas. 5:16).

Wholehearted church planters exercise this missional love language when they exercise prayer of dominant desire for the people they are called to reach.[6]

What is your missional love language? What is the love language of your church planting team? Are all of the love languages expressed in your church? To which of these are your immediate neighbors most receptive? How will you practice these in the place where you live?

Chapter 13

Marrying a Place and Its People

LINDA BERGQUIST

Remember, every place has people who love it. Find them.
Bring them together, ask them for their help.
Find out what is loveable about it and make it better.

—PETER KAGEYAMA[1]

A few years ago, Linda and her husband attended a dinner where a prominent evangelist spoke about loving a place. He encouraged pastors and other ministry leaders to love their city enough to do more than just flirt with her and consume her opportunities. "Marry her," he exhorted. That stuck in my mind. What does it mean to love a place so much that you invest your life there?

This chapter reflects on three aspects of place that affect church planters. First is the topic of how church planters choose where they will work and live and how that relates to their sense of calling (the courtship phase). Second, once a church planter and the planter's spouse determine that calling, there is an engagement phase with a marriage potential that is directly related to how the planter actually relates to that place. High engagement equals high hopes for lasting love. After the wedding is the work of marriage. As the marriage continues, one takes on the job of sustaining the relationship in ways that nourish it.

As readers consider this chapter, Linda and Allan want them to realize that marrying a city can mean staying in one place for a very long time, even forever. Consider Luke 10:6–7. When Jesus sent out seventy-two workers to the harvest fields, He gave very specific instructions: "If someone who promotes peace is there, your peace will rest on them; if not, it will return to you. Stay there, eating and drinking whatever they give you, for the worker deserves his wages. Do not move around from house to house."

Jesus told the seventy-two to *stay*, which was an undetermined time. However, it did not necessarily mean forever. In fact, verse 17 acknowledges that the sent ones all came back from their missions with joy. Some people are gifted to stay the long haul. Russ Cox started a church in Chula Vista, California, in 1987 and remains there as its founding pastor. Other people are gifted apostolically. That is to say, they are serial church planters who God gifts to go from place to place starting new churches. Our friend John Worcester is wired this way. He and his family have moved from Orange County, California, to Fort Worth, Texas, to Northern California, to San Diego, to Toronto, leaving churches behind everywhere they go. Patrick of Ireland is a classic example, and the apostle Paul is the very best example of apostolic gifting. However, it is important to know that when Paul moved on to the next place where he would start a church, he did at least two things. First, he raised up leaders to carry on the work he had started, and, second, he wrote love letters that kept him relationally and spiritually connected with people who lived in the places where he had started new churches. He committed to the peoples of the places where he traveled.

Choosing a Place and Its People

City expert Richard Florida wrote a book called *Who's Your City*. Believing that where to live is one of the most important decisions a person ever makes, he wrote the book to help people find a place that is right for them. Florida's work is mentioned here because church planters make important decisions about where to plant their lives, not just about where to plant churches. They choose to either stay where they are or move somewhere else based on a number of criteria. Indigenous planters are people who stay close to home, often because their lives are rooted in family and friends and work there. They stay where they are comfortable and because they have no real reason to go anywhere else. Missionary (cross cultural) church planters seek out other places where they see:

1. opportunities to reach more people who are not Christians,
2. where a specific people group lives,
3. where more paid job offerings appear available,
4. perceived needs for new churches,
5. an opportunity to join church planting teams,
6. openness to explore new worlds,
7. a chance to seek some kind of specialization, such as a church among artists in Oakland, surfers in San Diego, or oil workers in North Dakota's Bakken formation.

The significance of place that is both specific and local has been written about much in fields as diverse as philosophy, ecology, city planning, and architecture. Theologians and missionaries are rediscovering the concept too, for it is richly rooted in Scripture. Teacher/author/missiologist Sean Benesh writes:

Our theology of place has a direct bearing even on where we are drawn to minister and plant churches. If in our theological schemas, place is undervalued, or in this case various parts of the city are neglected, then there is a high likelihood of avoidance. That does not necessarily mean that everyone needs to pool and collect in the same parts of the city, but to instead realize that where we choose to live can be in some ways reflective of our theological assumptions of place.[2]

Benesh believes that the concept of calling is complex. People sense God's call to go to one place or another partially because of their own histories, their experiences, and how they are wired. They are more prepared to hear a call to one place over another. Allan and Linda have seen it over and over–eyes that leap when prospective planters discover a community that fits who they are and the future they imagine.

Falling in Love with a Place

In serious relationships, a person always detects something beautiful and special about the other–her hair, his voice, how she laughs, or the way he hums when he is cooking a gourmet meal for her. When people begin to love a place, they find particular things they love about it.

Linda loves San Francisco because of the shoe garden near the gardener's shed in Alamo Square Park and because it has an excellent public transportation system and because her immediate neighbors are Burmese, Chinese, African American, and Vietnamese.

Some love New York because the subway system gives them privy to watch families interact on the way to work and school each weekday and because it seems like just about everything there is famous or because they were born in New York.

Others love Oakland because it takes arts to the streets every first Friday and because it projects public films on a ten-thousand-square-foot wall on those same evenings.

Others love Boston because they attended college there along with one hundred thousand other college students and because of the ethos of colleges and universities such as MIT, Harvard, and Boston University. What do you love about your unique place, and what things make it special or lovely to you? Does a place have to be large and famous to create a love spot in your heart?

That Jesus wept over the city of Jerusalem (Jn. 11:35) is quoted often as a passage to show how much He loved cities. However, Jesus did not simply love cities in the abstract; He loved *His* city. This was the Jerusalem where:

1. His family visited each year for the Passover celebration;
2. He impressed temple teachers when He was twelve;

3. He healed a blind man at the pool of Siloam;
4. He taught the Lord's Prayer;
5. He entered on the back of a donkey to the sweet sounds of "Hosanna";
6. He celebrated the Last Supper with His disciples;
7. He prayed alone on its outskirts at Gethsemane at the foot of the Mount of Olives;
8. He was arrested, convicted, and crucified.

This was the place Jesus loved.

Linda's Story

When I was twenty years old, I visited San Diego over a long weekend. I was so drawn to that place that when I returned home, I immediately sold most of my belongings, packed the rest in the back of my 1958 Ford, and drove to San Diego. I stayed there for the next twenty-four years, except for a few years I spent in seminary. After seminary, I thought I was ready to go anywhere in the world, but I mostly wanted to practice what I had learned about church planting back home again, even in my home church. I eventually left San Diego only because I needed a new job.

Love changes the script for people and places. Children who are loved by their extended families, their teachers, and their neighbors flourish better throughout their whole lives than do children who never experience being loved. This is also true about cities. They flourish when their residents love them. When people love a place, it is almost inevitable that they love the people who live there. New parents are usually so enthralled with their infants that they are eager to share stories about them with anyone who will stop to listen. Have you ever noticed that newlyweds refer to their weddings as *the* wedding? Loving a community, a neighborhood, or a city also makes it easier to share stories with potential church planters and partner churches who, as a result, respond to that kind of affection for a place. Potential church planters find their places absolutely beautiful, and they want others to find them beautiful, too. As people learn to love the places where they live, their vision casting becomes contagious. They become more effective at recruiting church planters, partners, and teams; and they are generally more willing to sacrifice for the sake of those places.

Committing to a Place

Commitment is the next phase of a relationship. It signifies that you want to spend time with your beloved, get to know her, care about what it important to her. Her people become your people, and your people become hers. You serve one another, and you begin to strengthen the relationship in lasting ways. Here are some ways to say a firm "I do" to a place and to learn to know it well.

Be a Tourist

Explore it one neighborhood at a time. Shop, eat, bank, and walk one area at a time. After a while, move on to the next. Purchase tourist books, if there are any, and become familiar not only with regional icons (iconic place are easy to love), but explore the area's less known secrets, too. Remember that small towns and places that are new to you can be viewed from the perspective of a tourist, too.

Become a Tour Guide

A few months after associate church planting strategist Brook Ewbank moved to the Bay Area, she began taking city tours so that she could help others get to know her community too. She explored Chinatown, the Financial District, the murals of the Mission District, and more. Brook developed a working knowledge of her new home and subsequently began offering vision tours and urban immersion experiences to others. If helping others were not the goal of her learning, she may have taken much longer to know the Bay Area really well.

Use Public Transportation, Bike, or Walk

Being on the ground allows for a much more intimate experience with many towns and cities. Some places are more walkable than others, and some offer more efficient public transportation. Still others have more bicycle and pedestrian trails. Using these modes of getting around town helps residents experience their communities in fuller, deeper, and more whole ways. A homeless man was the street sociologist who first told Linda about the unofficial neighborhood version of San Francisco. He knew the city remarkably well because he was on its sidewalks day and night.

Learn about the History of Your Town or City

The Bergquists have a whole shelf of books about San Francisco, including tourist books, history books, cookbooks, and sociology books. People write about old cities, large cities, and well-known places, so many books are available to help us. What about smaller towns, though? Visit the town library, dig up archives, and sit under the tutelage of people who have lived there all of their lives.

See Your Town Through the Eyes of Its People

Meet elected officials and others who serve, such as police and firefighters. Take time to meet other Christian leaders, nonprofit leaders, business owners, artists, and activists. Meet diverse people of different ages, ethnicities, and socioeconomic backgrounds. Each has a different story and perspective.

Volunteer

A house church we know volunteers by helping new Bhutanese refugees transition to life in the United States. Because of their concern and compassion for people, they have become familiar to the national community of newcomers from Bhutan. When the greater Bhutanese community was looking for a city to hold a national soccer tournament, they chose a place near this house church and asked them to host it. The group now has the opportunity to share God's love with many Bhutanese.

Join the Parties

Whether you live in a place that throws a great annual rodeo or one that wins the Super Bowl, become a joiner. Root for the home team; read the local newspaper to know which high school teams place first in soccer. Attend fairs, festivals, and benefit concerts. The day the team that started Epic Church arrived in San Francisco to explore the possibility of planting a church, the city was celebrating the inauguration of a public official. They held a huge outdoor party with a large outdoor viewing screen. People booed and mocked the outgoing leader and wildly cheered for the person who was newly elected. The politics of the Epic team's hometowns was radically different. However, these visitors not only tolerated the differences; they also they fell in love with San Francisco that day.

Pray Incessantly

When Rick Curtis was ready to plant a church, his supervisor/coach suggested that he prayerwalk his community, knock on doors, and ask people, "How can we pray for you and your family?" Soon God led Rick to a neighbor two houses from where he lived who told him that a year earlier, God had specifically sent him there to help start a church.

The new church started small, but then attendance jumped without explanation.

Rick's mentor was curious. "Where did all of these people come from all of a sudden?" he asked. Rick noted that they had all come from within the three-block radius that his mentor had suggested that he prayerwalk. He talked about people who were just driving by and felt compelled to pull into the parking lot and visit the church. Do you suppose that this young church planter, who now holds a regional position in his denomination, advocates bathing church planting in *prayer*?

Linda has particular places where she loves to go to pray for her city, such as the highway that runs along the ocean, the peaks of certain hills that overlook the city, or traveling into San Francisco while driving across the Golden Gate Bridge. Praying for the city in these places not only gives her a wonderful view of the city from which to pray appreciatively, but also helps her to remember how beautiful God made her home and the loveliness of His vision for it.

Caring about a Sustainable Future

When people who are able to leave inheritances do so, they frequently will an amount to their grandchildren as well as their children. Sometimes they leave money to various community benefit organizations, or even to their pets. They do so because they care about the future of those who profit from their inheritances. Churches that care about their communities also want to pass along an inheritance because they love their communities, seek their welfare, and want them to thrive. God told the prophet Jeremiah, "Seek the peace and prosperity of the city to which I have carried you into exile. Pray to the LORD for it, because if it prospers, you too will prosper" (Jer. 29:7). Here are some ways that wholehearted church planters show long-term love to the places they love.

They Start Churches That Start Churches

Church planters realize that the churches they begin will not reach all of the geographies and people around them, so they develop Kingdom-oriented DNA by raising up generations of leaders who can extend the church's ministry to other peoples and places. In other words, they want to have children that bear their Kingdom resemblances, and they realize they are blessed to be a blessing. Recently Linda was in a launch service of a new church where the teaching pastor preached a stand-alone message about the church as community. He talked about serving one another, but no mention was made about serving the church by caring for the immediate neighborhood or beyond into the world. "Blessing" was addressed as the need for church members to receive God's blessings rather than how they are to be a blessing to others. The message was a little startling because most new churches we know are becoming more outwardly focused, possibly as a result of the missional church movement of this day.

They Practice Evangelistic Sustainability

By this we mean that instead of merely harvesting low-lying evangelistic fruit, churches that care about the future of a community also engage in sowing seed. They care about the harvest that will be reaped in the future, perhaps even by churches of other denominations. Strategies like mailing invitations to 25,000 homes and offering major seeker events are harvesting activities. Attractional type churches are exceptionally good at harvesting, but many never intentionally re-seed the unprepared soils of their communities. The work of starting churches among unreached people groups is a good example of sowing seed that may take years before experiencing a harvest.

They Model Long-term Stewardship for the Earth

Recycling is a good beginning, but can you imagine a completely paper-less church? This is one of the advantages of organic/simple churches most people never consider. For churches where buildings are indispen-sible, though, think in terms of what will last and what will use resources well. In denser areas, consider meeting close to public transportation lines or in walkable communities for the long-term good of the planet. After all, "The earth is the LORD's" (Ps. 24:1), and humans are called to cooperate with God in its care.

One of Oakland's newer sacred spaces is the Cathedral of Christ the Light, the mother church for 600,000 parishioners in the Catholic dio-cese. This stunning edifice was constructed from ordinary materials–glass, steel, concrete, and common Douglas fir. The cathedral was designed sus-tainably to last three hundred years, and built to be a connecting place between the cathedral and the city. Needless to say, the people of Oakland love their cathedral.

Church planters address the *shalom*–the peace of the place where you live and minister. Work to heal, and not harm, its land, for love has real physical implications, not just idealistic ones. How you live matters now, as well as in the long-term future, so invest well and bless the place God has given you to steward.

Practice these things, and in the end you will have lived out the "I do" that you promised to the place God gave you to cherish.

Chapter 14

Mutuality in Partnerships

ALLAN KARR

Sometimes the questions are complicated and the answers are simple.
                                                            –DR. SEUSS[1]

The Challenge of Partnerships

As I wrote this section of the book, a matter of fervent prayer occupied my life for a couple of weeks. A close friend of mine, who is an indigenous wholehearted church planting pastor in another country, had been arrested with two of his mentees, and was in prison for his faith. While he was teaching some disciples in his home, a mob had come into his home and attacked him and the people of his church. The local police came and arrested him and two others for what they said was protective custody. However, they kept them in jail for two weeks while they decided whether to file charges against them for converting people to Christ. Other local Christian leaders were very brave and went boldly to the police to ask for their release. As I was writing this paragraph, I got an e-mail stating that all three believers had been released from prison and no charges were filed. It was an occasion to pause and thank God for hearing the prayers of many people. No matter how it was resolved, we were asking for God's Kingdom to come and will to be done, on earth as it is in heaven. We celebrated this truth!

The reason I told that story is that, outside of the United States, wholehearted church planters encounter persecution for their faith and evangelism from their culture, their non-Christian faith communities, and their governments. In the case of my friends, they experienced persecution from all three in this one event.

However, in the United States, church planters usually have a much different experience. The culture and community are usually neutral out of apathy about the churches' efforts. The government is not arresting Christians for planting new churches. The government gives them official status to be a church and offers religious tax breaks for their activities. In the United States, the church planters often are "persecuted" by other believers in Jesus, other Christians. Often other local pastors are upset that a new church is starting in the territory they consider "their own," and feel a competitive angst about the presence of a new church option in their community. A new model that isn't traditional sometimes threatens some denominational workers. Some pastors, who are basically not involved, insert themselves into an artificially created controversy that is simply a difference in missiological preferences.

When I was praying about church planting for the first time in 1994, I contacted a denominational leader in a small metropolitan city in the western United States. The city had virtually doubled in size in the previous ten years, but very few, if any, new churches had been planted. I inquired about planting a new church in that city. The denominational leader told me that we didn't need to start a new church in the city until all the existing churches were full, and that at that time, many of the church buildings were nowhere close to being filled. God used that to direct me to the place I eventually planted a church, but I still remember the conversation with consternation. Even in my new city, my strongest opposition was from the pastor of a church in my own denomination for being too close to his church. There was even a "2 Mile Rule" on the books of our denomination that said no church could be planted within two miles of an existing church. We contested the missiological soundness of that rule, and it was overturned, but it caused negative emotions for many parties.

Some denominational leaders are upset about the model or worship style of the new church plant. Some Christians are concerned for fear of doctrinal differences. Some don't like the idea in principle or preference. In 2002, I was a full-time professor, and many of my students had been in mission fields overseas. I was teaching church planting classes, and my overseas students were asking many questions about house churches. I didn't have time resources to plant anything other than a bi-vocational model, and did not want to start a model dependent on lots of financial resources either. My wife and I learned about the relational model and were led to plant this model of church that was new to us. It was also new to many people in our denominational structures, so that for several years we lived in the tension of the resulting conflicts. God used that ultimately to teach me in some needed personal growth issues and to build my faith, but those experiences make it clear that this is an important topic to discuss for wholeheartedness in this context of church planting.

Church planters in the United States are often surprised at the amount of criticism, opposition, resistance, antagonism, and hostility they receive *from people they initially imagined would be supportive.* The truth is, many Christians support church planters, but a little opposition is often magnified in the context of intense emotions in the initial phases of a church plant. However, it must be noted that, in the United States, the criticism comes more from Christians, even partners, than from the unbelievers in the culture, community, or government.

With these realities in mind, this chapter is about how to apply wholeheartedness to the context of partnerships. Church planters need healthy caring relationships with their sponsoring churches, local partners, networks, and denominations. The principles of mutual wholeheartedness go in both directions in these relationships. Church planters need to relate in healthy ways to their contexts, and their partnering entities need to understand how to meet the needs of those who depend on their encouragement.

Healthy Caring Relationships

Local Partners

There are a variety of ways that planters can partner locally. One of the most common ways is in the use of a building. In our network of churches, we are trying to start models of churches that are less expensive. Some models of churches require a large start up and maintenance budget. While we need some churches like this, most often resources are not available to plant all the churches we need to plant if all the models require enormous budgets. My network has focused on trying to start models of churches that are less expensive. We cut the needed budgets by using bivocational and lay people extensively in church leadership. Borrowing a building from an existing church proves the biggest way to reduce the budget.

Many of the churches we start are non-English speaking, so we approach existing churches that own buildings and ask them to be local partners. Even though our church is the "sponsor" church, the other church can be a partner by donating the use of their building at times the partner is not currently using its facilities. Such partnerships can save tens of thousands of dollars a year in rental expenses and allow us to plant more churches.

We could plant hundreds of more churches a year in every state or province if existing churches would plant a new church in their building(s). Local partners can make a giant contribution to the Kingdom without adding significantly to their budgets. Such a partnership offers existing churches a great way to partner in wholehearted ways.

These kinds of partnerships require both parties to be considerate to each other. The host church needs to be willing to be flexible with schedules and tolerant of extra wear and tear requiring earlier updates to maintenance. The new congregation needs to be willing to train its people in proper control of their children and the cleanliness expectations of the host congregation. The new congregation needs to value the building even more than if it were their own. Many host churches have to get used to sharing kitchens with people whose cuisine is different, producing odors foreign to them. New congregations need to learn the culture of the host congregation and work to accommodate the issues as they arise. We have had to deal with these issues frequently with Hispanic, Karen, and Korean new congregations being hosted in borrowed buildings. This requires wholeheartedness from both sides of the partnership, but can be a great blessing to both churches, and to the Kingdom of God.

Churches can partner in other ways.. For example, local churches in the Bay Area of California are always helping the mission work we are doing with the refugees from Afghanistan in Fremont. Local partners can provide food for events, help with tutoring and mentoring, and open their benevolence pantries to the people we are trying to love in new churches. A little creativity produces literally countless ways for churches to be wholehearted partners to new churches.

Sponsoring Churches

For the last eighteen years, sponsoring churches have been part of my everyday life, whether as a recipient of being sponsored or being the one sponsoring. Also, through my teaching and mobilizing of missionaries, I have a vast array of experiences with churches that decide to sponsor new churches. Most sponsoring churches are sincere in helping a new church be planted, and give generously of their financial and human resources. Most are legitimately Kingdom-hearted. Some, however, have self-serving motives, a spirit of control, or unrealistic expectations.

My family and team planted a traditional seeker-sensitive attractional model church in 1995 helped by an outstanding sponsoring church. They were empowering, encouraging, and thoughtful, following the leadership of the senior pastor Rick Ferguson[2] and the Minister of Missions, Duane Arledge. Our sponsoring church was always supportive of our plant in Castle Rock. In 2002, after I was a full-time missionary professor, we started a new church with a different bi-vocational vision. The same church sponsored us again. This church has since become the measuring stick by which other sponsoring churches are compared.

A later chapter discusses the many caring characteristics of healthy partnering churches. Here we must simply underline that to be healthy, these partnership should be mutually beneficial. The church plant may seem to benefit more, but much Kingdom fruit and blessing become visible when the church plant is reciprocal. Partnering churches have hopes and expectations from the new church plant.

Networks

In 2002, my family planted a church called *Ethne Church Network*. The name reflected a vision more than a reality. The vision was that we wanted to reach all the people groups in our community, and that the new church(es) would reflect the diversity so characteristic in the Denver, Colorado, metro area. We also envisioned creating a network, a term that caused confusion in my denomination at that time. We knew we wanted to grow our church, but believed in theory that there were at least two ways to grow. One way to grow would be to outgrow our living room in our home and then look to rent or borrow a bigger space to accommodate more people. That way required a growing budget and time requirements for the leadership team. The second way to grow would be to reproduce. We could and did ask God to raise up new leaders from the harvest, train them, and then release them to start new autonomous churches. These new churches would be independent, autonomous churches, but would be connected relationally to the "network." Our network is now over ten years old and is still growing and evolving. It reflects a diverse network of churches, with many ethnicities and language groups of our city represented. In a given week, over 1000 people are part of the faith communities that represent all the autonomous churches of the Ethne Church Network.

A year or so after Ethne Church Network started, we decided we wanted to become a recognized church in our denomination, a process that required we start with being credentialed in our local regional association of churches. We submitted our paperwork, and the meeting was scheduled with the "Credentials Committee." We went to the meeting, as did another church seeking to be credentialed. They were a restart of a church that had died, but they were using the same small church building for the new church. They were a very traditional church, an attractional model meeting in a church building. They were actually smaller numerically than our church, even though we met in my home. They met with the committee first. Within about fifteen minutes or so, the committee approved them.

Ethne Church Network went before the committee, which frankly did not seem adversarial. Indeed they appeared inclined to be an advocate for our new church to be approved. However, they asked questions for almost two hours, only to decide we needed a follow-up meeting with many more associational pastors at the table. The issues had nothing to do with theology or doctrine. It had to do with being a church meeting in a home and having the vision of being a network. The term "Network" in our church's name confused most of the traditionally minded people who limited church planting to only one church, excluding any vision of many autonomous churches.

They asked, "Are you starting a church or a network of churches?" I answered, "Yes." We envisioned having a relational church that would meet in our home and then become the sponsoring church for many other new churches that would be tied together relationally. For starters, the question arose, "Can a church that meets in a house be the sponsoring church for a new church plant?" For most of the world, that is a silly question; but for traditionally minded American church culture people, it was a paradigm buster. A few weeks later, we had our follow-up meeting with a few more people present and some more questions. In the end, the association approved our request to be credentialed and welcomed us into the association. However, the unresolved "network" issue continues to be confusing and misunderstood by most traditionalists to this day. Yet we have observed that many wholehearted church planters strongly desire to have the relational encouragement and accountability that networks provide.

How does a healthy "network" operate? In our current church planting culture, networks are becoming quite popular. Some are based on affinity or shared values, such as Acts 29.[3] Others are more regionally based, like *Bay Area Church Planting*,[4] started by a team of people led by my co-author Linda Bergquist, for the planters in the San Francisco Bay Area. Some networks are based on a ministry strategy, like Set Free or the Willow Creek Association. Some networks require a membership fee, and some are strictly held together by relationships. Healthy networks are the ones in which all parties are satisfied that the resources it takes to connect are mutually beneficial. Some church planters are willing to pay to be in a network simply for the credibility they perceive from being in the network. Some networks provide mentoring and coaching by the lead planter or the team.

Networks provide prayer support, emotional support, encouragement, friendship, and a sense of belonging to something bigger than just the single church plant. They also offer a source of information of current church trends and news. In a past era, denominations served this role, but in an era in which loyalty to a denomination is waning, networks have emerged to meet this need for many church leaders. Networks are another way many church planters develop partnerships. This trend seems to be growing in popularity, and the networks are evolving to meet the emerging needs of the planters.

Mutuality in the Wholehearted Church Planter

Most partnerships are entered into because of a perceived benefit to each party. Church planting partnerships differ from strict business partnerships because of the concept of the Kingdom of God. In the Kingdom, the benefits are not always able to be measured to ensure equal benefits to all parties. That being said, the expectations of partnerships go in both directions. Donors, sponsoring churches, networks, and denominational organizations have hopes and needs in the relationships they have with church planters. Church planters have the responsibility to understand the needs of their partners and agree to attempt to meet those needs, or have the integrity to opt out of the partnership before it starts.

A disappointing reality is that some church planters have abused their partnerships. Some planters entered into a partnership to have access to start up funding, only to dissolve the partnership the minute the funding structure expires. The denomination, sponsoring church, or network then feels used, abused, and burned. The actions of one selfish planter damage the relationships with many new planters in the future. In partnerships, everyone could and should be happy, but quite commonly partnerships have been a source of frustration and discouragement. We are hoping that partners and planting teams are wholehearted in their relationships with each other.

Planters need to consider the needs and expectations of their partners.. Many sponsoring churches are very excited to reproduce and feel as if they are contributing to the Kingdom of God beyond the scope of their own local church. I have observed that a key to experiencing a healthy mutuality lies in good communication, especially as the partnership is covenanted. Understanding the mutuality in the relationship from the beginning of the partnership is of absolute importance.

As the partnership matures, the need to communicate on an ongoing basis is key to the mutual satisfaction with the partnership. The relationship with partners can mature over time to be a rich source of joy for all parties. The lead planter and team feel affirmed, encouraged, and resourced. The church plant feels secure in being part of a bigger relationship and feels nurtured by the relationships. The partnering organization feels joy in being able to contribute to a mission of expanding the Kingdom of God. Denominations were started to cooperate for missions and fellowship. Networks emerged to encourage churches that share affinity and trust. Healthy sponsoring churches want to reproduce for the same reasons that the Antioch church in Acts 13 sent out Paul and Barnabas as missionaries. Partnerships are designed to be mutual. Church planters and partnering organizations need to be wholehearted in their relationships with each other. We are hoping that in the future the majority of stories we hear of partnerships are mutually beneficial and relationally rich, and that the negative experiences are the rare exceptions.

Section IV: Knowing and Loving Self

Chapter 15

The Self-Aware Church Planter

LINDA BERGQUIST

It takes heroic humility to be yourself and to be nobody but the man, or the artist, God intended you to be. –THOMAS MERTON[1]

When Linda's daughter was young, she took dance lessons and performed in the San Francisco Youth Ballet. Each of the nine years she performed, her practice became more rigorous and her steps more graceful. She was an amateur, but those who loved her most were mesmerized by her performances. What do you suppose it must be like for God to watch His children engage in the dance of Kingdom ministry? He does not seek perfection; He just wants to see us dance. He loves seeing our spirits become strong through doing what He created us to do.

The book of Ephesians provides some of the most exquisite dance music ever imagined. We are "His workmanship, created in Christ Jesus for good works" (Eph. 2:10, NASB). Individually and collectively we are His, uniquely formed to bring glory to our Maker. God made each of us differently, gifted us differently, and shaped us with unique sets of experiences out of which we serve Him and one another in love. Again in Ephesians, "Christ himself gave the apostles, the prophets, the evangelists, the pastors and teachers, to equip his people for works of service" (Eph. 4:11–12a). Church planters start new churches out of all of the leadership gifts listed here.

This chapter is meant as a rallying cry. We want you to believe that God made, shaped, and gifted you beautifully with unique sets of experiences out of which you can serve Him and others. Linda and Allan want church planters to know themselves and to minister out of a healthy assessment of their own spiritual gifts, personalities, strengths, and work styles. Conversely, we want them to acknowledge their own weaknesses and not try to live into someone else's vision or calling. We also aim to encourage more people to start new churches, and encourage more existing churches to trust the God-shaped call in many wonderfully ordinary people to plant new gospel-centered communities.

Four presuppositions guide our thinking.

1. It honors God when we function in accordance with His design for our lives.
2. People with various spiritual gifts, backgrounds, and personalities can plant churches.
3. Team church planting is normative in Scripture.
4. Leadership can be learned.

God Chooses and Uses All Kinds of People

Ephesians 4 Gifts

"There is no one alive who is youer than you," reads the familiar Dr. Seuss book *Happy Birthday To You.* God uses all kinds of "yous" to start churches. First, He calls some who minister primarily to people outside of the church. Those with the spiritual gift of apostleship plant multiple churches. The word *apostolos* means "sent," so apostolic leaders lead the body of Christ into their calling as the *sent people of God.* Mature apostolic leaders may catalyze church planting for whole regions, and even across regions and people groups. Prophets are truth tellers who are tuned in to the voice of God and are able to speak into cultures in ways that turn people's hearts towards Him. Churches are started out of repentant new followers of Jesus. Evangelists lead people to Christ and form discipleship groups. Churches emerge from that core. The Church needs to pay attention to raising up and releasing prophets and evangelists if revival and church planting movements are really going to happen.

People with shepherding and teaching gifts usually minister to people inside of the church, although a growing number of them also use these spiritual gifts to reach out to the world. Shepherds are pastoral types who care for people. They need the assistance of apostles, prophets, or evangelists to help draw people from the outside to the inside of the community of faith. Sometimes they use attractional methodologies that substitute for these other Ephesians 4 gifts; for example, radio broadcasts or mass mailers allow them to invite communities to special events. Some pastoral leaders take responsibility for whole neighborhoods. They establish a presence by taking on the role of chaplains or parish priests, whether or not people attend the churches they lead. In time, this too draws people towards the gospel and into churches.

Finally, church planters with outstanding teaching gifts can gather and lead people who are hungry for scriptural teaching and edification. They often apply their teaching gifts by incorporating videos of their messages on their websites or by advertising message series with wide public appeal. Linda and Allan believe that the Church's neglect of apostolic gifts in particular, and, secondarily, of prophetic and evangelism gifts, has helped make attractional methodologies as popular as they are today. What would the field of church planting look like today if the apostles, prophets, and evangelists among us were truly mobilized?[2]

God Uses Ordinary People

God could have called Moses to lead the people out of slavery when he sat in Pharaoh's courts, but He waited until Moses was tending sheep in the desert. David was a common shepherd boy who grew up to be the king of Israel. Amos, another shepherd, took care of sycamore-fig trees before he became a prophet. A young virgin named Mary became the mother of Jesus, the Messiah, who learned the trade of a carpenter. Jesus then called out a band of followers that included fishermen, a tax collector, and others of lowly birth. The apostle Paul was born into a more privileged life, but he recognized that God works through whomever He desires:

> Brothers and sisters, think of what you were when you were called. Not many of you were wise by human standards; not many were influential; not many were of noble birth. But God chose the foolish things of the world to shame the wise; God chose the weak things of the world to shame the strong. God chose the lowly things of this world and the despised things—and the things that are not—to nullify the things that are, so that no one may boast before him (1 Cor. 1:26–29)

Dave and Jon Ferguson wrote an inspiring book called *Exponential: How You and Your Friends Can Start a Missional Church Movement.* They begin the book with this challenge: "Every movement starts with one person. When you and your friends become apprentices of Jesus, you will follow in his footsteps and say to others, 'Come follow me.'" Throughout the book they emphasize the reproduction of individuals, leaders, groups, churches, and movements, using any ordinary person who is grabbed by God's heart.[3]

Who Is a Church Planter?

Craig Van Gelder and Dwight J. Zscheile note, "Prevailing models of church planting leadership often draw more from business entrepreneurship and institution building than from the practices of cultivating communities of discipleship, discernment, and witness."[4] While certainly God uses these kinds of church planters, is there room for those who are not even remotely business entrepreneurs?

From our perspective, the kind of people who plant churches should have a different set of common characteristics. By now, you know that we refer to the distinctives of a Luke 10:27 call. First, these kinds of church planters know God well enough to realize that He is a gracious sending God, one who desires everyone to respond to His love. They trust Christ enough to believe in His central message about the Kingdom of God and to listen for the Holy Spirit's direction in their lives. They want to be in His presence. They know that whenever the Spirit whispers, "go," He will also prepare the way. They are aware that they can do nothing in their own strength, but that in Christ all things are possible, including planting a church. Can you imagine yourself taking on the character and mission of Christ in the world? Milfred Minatrea writes, "Intimacy with God results in leaders being fashioned into His likeness, recreated in His image. Their minds are consumed with the purposes of God and bringing Him glory."[5]

Second, these kinds of church planters love people and have a special concern for those to whom they have been sent. They do not want "anyone to perish, but everyone to come to repentance" (2 Pet. 3:9). They also love the followers of Jesus in their midst, and they want to see them flourish. They realize that it makes the Father glad to see his children enjoying one another and that the family of God is meant to live well together. Loving God *and* loving people is the soil out of which missional type leaders are born and raised.

Third, wholehearted church planters believe enough in the transformational power of the gospel that they trust God to work through them despite their own limitations and their weaknesses. Neil Cole observed that the apostle Paul grew in self-awareness over the years: "In his earlier writings, he refers to himself as the equal to the most eminent of apostles (2 Cor. 12:11). Later he writes that he is least of the Saints (Eph. 3:8). In one of his last writings he calls himself the foremost of all sinners (1 Tim. 1:15)."

Cole notes that Paul was not becoming more sinful, but that the longer and closer he walked with God, the more aware he was of his own sinful nature.[6]

Assessing Church Planters

Recently Linda spoke at a church planting conference in a small mid-America city. When she mentioned church planter assessments, one participant seemed especially interested and asked good questions. Linda and Allan believe that formal assessments are best used to help determine how a candidate fits into the church planting process, not to determine whether an individual can plant a church or not. Assessments can help potential planters think about what style of church they might consider starting, what kind of team with what kinds of spiritual gifts would complement their own, how their strengths and weaknesses would work in the plant, and where they might plant. Many denominations and church planting training centers have on-line pre-assessments and also offer full church planter assessments. Any search engine can be used to find more information.

People and organizations who support church planting have a right to look for particular capacities over others, to choose planters with traits that match local visions and needs, and to fund whomever they feel called to fund. The conference participant who asked Linda about assessments pointed out that it was especially difficult to recruit church planters to smaller towns like hers. She acknowledged that they would most likely need to develop a system for raising up leaders. She said her denomination was not necessarily looking for superstars; they just needed a few godly people with the courage to plant a church. Linda agreed with her that there would never be enough churches started if only people who scored really high in standard assessments qualified to plant churches. We need to be careful about using the expression, "This or that person is not a church planter." That is God's job.

Common Church Planting Characteristics

The Gift of Vision

Many people in the church planting field recognize a few characteristics as being essential to any kind of church planting. At the top of the list is the capacity to formulate a vision and to communicate it to others. However, few people are real visionaries, regardless of how they are rated by assessment tools. Visionary people have the capacity for future orientation and for some positive, hopeful idea about what a new future or new direction might be like. Linda and Allan's experiences with church planters convince them that people find ways to start and grow strong churches and church planting networks even when no classic visionary type church planters are available. Here are three ways with which we are familiar:

1. People with planning skills can take someone else's vision and create a plan that helps bring the vision to fruition. They do not need to be the creator of the vision to know how to help others to fulfill it. Strategic planners can sometimes go to bed at night with a problem in their minds and wake up in the morning with a full-blown plan for implementing a solution. Visionaries need strategic planners, and planners need visionaries, but not many can fulfill both roles with excellence except through dependency on the Spirit of God.

2. Church planters whose strengths fit into prevailing paradigms of church planting can make those paradigms work, even if they are not visionary leaders. They simply follow the playbooks. This is actually the case for many people who start traditionally structured churches. The more clear, prescribed, and formulaic the church planting paradigm, the more transferable it is. In the last several decades, numerous church planting conferences, books, boot camps, and websites have codified the process to the extent that planting traditional churches has become highly replicable.

   On the other hand, only a limited amount of such materials aim at people who plant simple/organic/house churches, since these are generally more fluid. Three resources come to mind: (a) Neil Cole's *Raising Leaders for the Harvest* (especially Life Transformation

Groups), (b) Felicity Dale's *Getting Started: A Practical Guide to Church Planting*, and (c) T4T: *A Discipleship Re-Revolution* by Steve Smith and Ying Kai. The T4T (training for trainers) approach includes a clear mentoring model that helps church planters to experience, not just read about, the paradigm. It is quite explicit in its methodology. We are all interested to see how the growing simple church movement in North America applies it to evangelism and church planting.

3. Implementing God's vision instead of one's own is essential. This means that instead of a visionary church planter determining a direction for the new church, the planter listens and waits for God's voice, direction, and empowerment. Church planters need to restore the priority of God's vision that people too often replace with their own big ideas. The skill set here is wholeheartedly knowing and loving God. Does this seem too simplistic? It is not meant to be, for hearing God's voice comes as the result of intimately and faithfully walking with Him. Wholehearted church planters do not need to be people of great vision; they just need to be people of great faith who know that ultimately God's vision for His Church matters. So where are you? A visionary? A strategic implementer? A good follower of existing patterns? A person whose life is intentionally oriented around a Luke 10:27 call?

Leadership Capacity

Leadership capacity is the single greatest pushback Linda and Allan received from others regarding the thesis of this book. "Not everyone is a leader," many said. Some insisted that leaders are born, not made. We have three basic responses. First, almost everyone can lead *something*–a nuclear family, a friendship group, a work project, a neighborhood group, a gang, or a Bible study in a convalescent home all count. The *degree* of leadership ability is the real issue, not the presence of it. Different kinds of churches need different kinds of leaders, and it is important to know one's self well enough to know where you fit.

Second, Linda and Allan believe that "teamship" is the primary biblical model of church planting. When God grants leadership gifts–apostles, prophets, evangelists, shepherds, and teachers–he does not expect any one person to fulfill all of these roles at once. The Bible records a Paul *and* Barnabas, a Paul *and* Silas, a Barnabas *and* John Mark, a group of *twelve* disciples, and *seventy-two* people Jesus sent out in teams of *two*. Good teams complement one another's strengths and weaknesses.

In addition to the above reasons for engaging teams, more people will be blessed and released to plant churches as they work in teams. Linda knows a woman who is currently serving a two-year missionary term in a church planting context. The young woman asked a denominational leader for advice about what kind of local missions work she might become involved in after her two-year term was completed. He told her to come back to him again when she had a ring on her finger. She was devastated. While this woman theologically agreed with her denomination's position about female senior pastors, she wanted to find a way that she could work on a church planting team as a volunteer. She simply wanted to find a way to make an impact in God's kingdom. Even those with very conservative interpretations of new Christians, singles, and/or women serving in ministry are often willing to bless their work in church planting teams. The use of teams in church planting ministries serves to multiply the church's potential to reach out and helps release more people for mission.

Our third response is grounded in the personal and spiritual development of wholehearted church planters. Because they walk with God, they learn wisdom and become increasingly capable of making good decisions that serve the people they lead. Because they love people and sacrifice on their behalf, people follow them and want to "play" on their teams. People trust wholehearted people who model Romans 5:5 in ways that affect lives: "God's love has been poured out into our hearts through the Holy Spirit, who has been given to us." As they continue to abide in Christ and as other wholehearted people mentor them, their own leadership capacity develops beyond what they imagined. Even the most unlikely can become spiritual leaders of new churches. Are you able to notice some growth in your own leadership abilities as you learn to walk closer to God and people?

Communication Skills

Communication skills here include not only preaching and teaching skills, but also e-mail, cell phone messaging, and various forms of social media. It is vital to learn how to communicate with people in the modes with which they are most comfortable. Every kind of church needs to take the Word of God seriously, but preaching does not necessarily need to be the central platform of all churches. Shared teaching is also an option, especially in simple, missional forms of church communities. Even in more traditional churches, preaching can be supplemented by video, drama, and other forms of communication that can help a speaker convey a message. A bi-vocational pastor who is new to preaching leads a certain church plant. The church meets in a fantastic location for which it pays only a pittance rental fee. They spend no money on advertising or salaries, but have gathered a small group of people who are learning to love one another. Meanwhile, the planter is learning to preach. Eventually the church will reach out to a wider network, but for now, they are in no rush to make that happen. They are willing and financially able to allow their pastor to take the time he needs to become a better up-front communicator.

Church planters find it important to learn how to communicate vision to those who partner with new churches. Scripture offers options. Moses, who was "slow of speech and tongue," asked God to send someone else to share what God wanted him to communicate. God told Moses to delegate the task to his brother Aaron and promised that he would help both brothers with the task. This arrangement did not seem to detract from Moses' leadership (Ex. 4:10–14). Moses eventually learned to communicate without Aaron's help. Paul offered another solution—relying on the Spirit to empower his words: "My message and my preaching were not with wise and persuasive words, but with a demonstration of the Spirit's power" (1 Cor. 2:4). Ask a few trusted friends to help you evaluate your communication style, critique your strengths and weaknesses, and help you know if you are really connecting with people. Ask God to demonstrate His power through you.

Relational Intentionality

Church planters who love being with people are good for new churches. Some operate out of spiritual gifts such as encouragement, hospitality, service, and mercy; but they also rely on team members with these gifts. Some church planters are better with tasks than they are with people. They have long lists of work to accomplish. Instead of including others in those tasks, they withdraw from people to get the job "done right" themselves. Others are so relationally oriented that they neglect tasks so they can spend more time with people.

The subtitle of this section, "Relational Intentionality," is borrowed from a chapter in Ed Stetzer and Thom Rainer's book *Transformational Church.* They write that some people are just naturally relational, with no particular pattern of intentionality. They also describe an opposite kind of person who is a "highly intentional achiever": "This person has skill with people but often sees individuals as part of the bigger picture. Intentional people...are visionaries who see the masses but not individuals. They are as passionate about tasks as the relational person is about relationships. Thus the achiever sees people as a way to achieve."[7] Which are you? Are you an achiever, a relational person, or are you more an intentional mix of both? Who can help you with this challenge and complement your natural capacities?

Church planters who love people also know how to relate to people who do not attend church or who do not profess faith in Christ. They know how to break through the obstacles that are barriers to their faith and how to spend time with people on their own "turf." They are incarnational in their communities and wherever else God calls them. Alan Roxburgh and Fred Romanuk, writing about missional leaders, claim that they take the Incarnation of Jesus quite seriously. Roxburgh and Romanuk write, "In the Incarnation, we discern that God is always found in what appears to be the most godforsaken of places–the most inauspicious of locations, people, and situations. God seems to be present where there is little or no expectation."[8] Incarnation is because God so loved the world. Incarnation is also characteristic of wholehearted church planters.

Passion

Church planting requires an enormous amount of just plain hard work. For this reason, most assessments frame questions that help discern the potential planter's drive or intrinsic motivation. Even when the work-load is shared with a team, the task is time consuming and sometimes even overwhelming. It is one thing to have a superior work ethic–some people seem to be born for hard work. It is a completely different thing to be motivated out of passion for Jesus and a life centered on the Great Commandment. Wholehearted church planters are people on a mission. Whether or not they seem born for high commitment and hard work, they become more focused and work more energetically just because they care so much. Because prayer fuels their work, the results are deeper, more abundant, and more sustainable. Great Commandment people are Great Commission people. May their tribe increase.

Chapter 16

Healthy Organizational Partnerships

ALLAN KARR (WITH KENNY MOORE)

Paradigm-busting missionaries in the nineteenth century gave much of our best current missiology to us. Perhaps we are tempted to think that in the twenty-first century we are creatively advancing in missiological strategy. In truth the best current missiology incorporates the same principles Paul taught to us, principles many missionaries throughout the history of Christendom have rediscovered. The rediscovery of biblical principles in missiology gives sound principles to wholehearted church planters as we consider the principles of healthy organizational partnerships. Just as these principles were counter-cultural in the mission context a hundred years ago, these ideas may challenge the status quo thinking in the twenty-first century as we consider the role of healthy partnerships in church planting.

The Nevius Principles

John Livingston Nevius provides one example of a paradigm buster that challenged the status quo of mission organizational partnerships with biblical principles. His ideas are summarized in a book of his writings published six years after his death.[1] Nevius and his wife were missionaries in China in the late nineteenth century. His mission ideas are responsible for the "3 Self" strategy of church planting ecclesiology present today in China and now known globally. Just before he died, Nevius went to Korea and taught his principles in almost virgin mission soil. The seed of his ideas took root without the weeds of a century of Western missiological ideas presenting challenges when a change in strategy is required. Nevius taught these principles for two weeks in Korea. His principles formed the foundation of the great Presbyterian movement of church planting that took root in that country starting the last decade of the nineteenth century. Nevius's strategy provides a sound missiological platform when considering how wholehearted church planters should engage in healthy organizational partnerships.

In China, Nevius pointed out that Western missionaries had come to the people groups in China and started the practice of providing vocational funding for indigenous leaders. Nevius explained the danger to the health of the mission of the Kingdom of God when the mission agency paid the indigenous leaders to be pastors of the new churches.

Charles Allen Clark created the standard nine-principle summary of the Nevius Method:

1. Widespread itinerant personal evangelism by the missionary;
2. Self propagation, that is, every believer as an evangelist and teacher of someone, as well as a learner, a model called layering;
3. Self-government, where unpaid believers lead their own individual churches; circuit helpers (paid by locals) aid these local believers by travelling from church to church, functioning as elder but unable to administer sacraments; later, paid pastors replace circuit helpers once the church is able to support its own pastor;
4. Self-support—believers build their own chapels, each group contributes to paid helpers' salary, schools receive only partial subsidy, and no pastors of single churches paid by foreign funds;
5. Systematic Bible study through a system of classes for biblical education of all believers;
6. Strict church discipline;
7. Co-operation and union with other bodies;
8. Noninterference in lawsuits;
9. General helpfulness in economic life problems of the people.[2]

Organizational Funding Practices

In the early twenty-first century, we are seeing the practice of salary funding for church planters as a rampant strategy in the recent emphasis of church planting in the United States and the areas of established church organization. Nevius was supported as a catalytic church planting missionary, paid as a missionary with foreign funds. His argument was not that there should be no mission dollars ever spent to share the gospel in spiritual harvest fields. His principle of "self-support" is that no *indigenous* church planters should be supported by *foreign* dollars. That principle means a healthy church plant funds ministers from local church resources divided by local congregation decisions based on what the local congregation can support. If mission agency dollars pay pastors, the pastors become addicted to the funding source, ultimately crippling the new church. In a domestic church plant we see the danger of this being played out repeatedly. Our culture of ministry feels that the church planter should be employed full time in the ministry. Partnership dollars consistently make this budget possible as a start up strategy, but after a couple of years or more the funding source dries up, leaving the new church crippled and often resentful. The church plant then limps along into the future at best, or folds as a worst-case scenario, a result we see far more than we like to admit.

For some reason, we can see that foreign organizational dollars damage the mission in "majority world" missions[3], but find it difficult to apply the same principles to church plants in the United States or Canada. It is quite counter-cultural to many of our current organizational partnership practices. If we start a new church not addicted to outside funding, it will start slower and be more challenging in the beginning. Later, as the church matures and decides how to spend their offerings, the church is generally much stronger and healthier, ready to move into the future as a strong presence of the Kingdom of God in their community.

Wedding Gifts for the Bride of Christ

What is a healthy alternative to salary funding? Partner organizations can bless a new church plant with some seed funds to get started, much like many cultures do for a newlywed couple. When a bride and groom get married, they register their needs; and then their family and friends bless them with things needed to start a new life together. It would not be healthy to the newlywed couple to give them a salary to pay their monthly expenses. If they can't afford to be married, they wait until their circumstances make it feasible, or until they can tolerate the struggle it sometimes takes to start a new life together. A new church is the Bride of Christ, and He is the groom. We can celebrate new churches with honeymoon gifts, but we damage churches when we start them off with salary funding. In Nevius's principles, outsiders' gifts included help with discipleship training and partial funding of schools. Nevius's proposed principles were not well received over a hundred years ago, but they are now seen as sound missiological principles in a foreign context. I am proposing they are universally sound, including domestic church planting contexts.

One day I was discussing this funding issue with my mentor Kenny Moore. It is a common topic of conversation between us. Kenny always tells me many stories (mostly about horses or the lumber business). On this particular day he told me about a meeting he attended where many church planting partners were discussing strategy. One person in the meeting was bemoaning the decrease of partnership mission dollars available to pay salaries of church planters. He asked, "What is going to happen if all the partnership money dries up? We will never plant any more churches!"

Kenny replied, "I think we will plant more churches than ever before." Explaining his comment, he said that if God wants to plant a church, then the planter and the church will rely on God. When they don't have the false safety net of outside salary funding, the movement of reproduction will be healthier and more prolific than it would be if we only planted as funds from outside the community allowed. We will plant models of churches we can afford, and our box of acceptable models will be expanded. Healthy disciples will make healthy churches, and they will take ownership of the wholehearted commission of Christ to make disciples, starting with their own Jerusalem, and then to the ends of the earth.

Roland Allen

Roland Allen was a groundbreaking missiologist whose career followed Nevius's. Allen also challenged the partnership status quo. An English Anglican priest from the nineteenth into the twentieth century, Allen became a missionary to China, and then to Kenya in his later career. The Boxer rebellion in 1900 interrupted his missionary efforts in China, as many indigenous Christians and missionaries were killed or imprisoned. In painful times, Allen contemplated the role of mission partners among the indigenous culture.

Many mission agency leaders despised Roland Allen because his ideas often diametrically opposed the accepted practices in missions. "[It] was Allen's insights into the expansion of the Church that sometimes equated him as being a prophet, a revolutionary, a radical, or a troublemaker."[4] Roland Allen's 1912 classic work, *Missionary Methods: St. Paul's or Ours?* criticized and proposed revolutionary changes in the ways that mission agencies engaged indigenous cultures. "Allen advocated that the missionary methods of the Apostle [Paul] were not antiquated but rather to be applied to missionary endeavors in any day and time."[5] Allen proposed that paying clergy from outside sources was detrimental to the mission. He believed in making disciples of indigenous leaders and in trusting the leaders to develop the churches as God directed.

In the spirit of Allen's work, I would propose that organizational partnerships that have at their root a desire to *control* the church planter do not form a healthy partnership. Such partnerships are not healthy missiology nor are they relationally and spiritually healthy to the mission of the new church.

"The following year saw Allen's publication of *Missionary Principles.* In this work Allen advocated that the indwelling Holy Spirit provides the missionary zeal."[6] Just like Roland Allen, I would propose that the principles that we apply to missionary work in overseas cultures should be applied to the mission work we do in church planting in domestic efforts. Wholehearted church planting is not simply following a formula: finding a niche in the demographic that needs a new church, finding a place to meet, marketing the new plant to the community, and opening the doors to try to attract a crowd. That is how new businesses start, but it is not a biblical model of missions. Too often our organizational partnerships are trying to equip planters in this strategy.

The Funding Trap

Today many popular missiological partnering practices too often violate Nevius and Allen's principles of planting healthy churches. Far too many church plants are crippled, dependent on the start up salary funds that are being requested and given. Some would argue that certain models of church planting are not possible without a large investment of start up funding and salary funding to allow the planter to work vocationally full time on the plant. However, the same arguments were being made in nineteenth-century China, and Nevius and Allen pointed out the institutional danger of that strategy. My mentor and prayer partner Kenny Moore is a long-time church planting strategist. In 1996, while I was a church planter in Colorado, Kenny wrote a letter to our denominational leadership arguing the cruelty of salary funding of church planters. That same year our state had outlawed the use of leg traps for wildlife harvesting because of the cruel nature of the method. In that context Kenny wrote, "Colorado voted to outlaw leg traps because of the cruel nature of the damage inflicted upon the animal. From personal experience, I know that traps *maim, cripple, and even sometimes kill their victims.* At the risk of hyperbole, I am suggesting that our use of our mission funds for salaries is a trap that is debilitating our mission work..."[7] In the spirit of Roland Allen and Nevius, Kenny pointed out how damaging the funding has been for a majority of church plants historically. In the context of a family of partnerships, we are rearing our new churches to be dependent on institutional funding, and growing up with a crippled ability to be self-supporting, self-governing, and self-propagating. Far too often, we are planting with an unhealthy partnering strategy, and birthing new churches that are crippled, maimed, and even die because of the partnering funding trap. Maiming and crippling is not a desired outcome of wholehearted organizational partnerships.

Partnerships as "Family"

As a pastor, I don't believe that making disciples ends when a new follower of Jesus makes a profession of faith. I teach and live that the profession is just the beginning. At our church, we tell our mentees a story about being a family. The new church is a new family. The church is the bride, and Jesus is the groom. What if, in my actual family, we adopted an infant, brought the new baby home, and told her, "We are so glad you are in our family. Here is where you sleep. Here is the kitchen where all the food is located if you are hungry. Here is where you go to the toilet and take your baths. We are so glad you are in our family now!"

What if we said that to the new baby and left her to fend for herself? The new baby would suffer and die, since no one was caring for her. Sometimes as an institution of church we employ that same strategy to new "baby" Christians. They make a profession of faith and get baptized. We say welcome and tell them about the programs of the church. Then far too often we leave them to fend for themselves. Many of them struggle in their new faith and church.

New Christians need care, but so do new churches. Church plants share similar characteristics. New churches thrive best in the context of a loving, nurturing family. Part of being wholehearted in this context is being a nurturing extended family as an organizational partner.

In the context of thinking like a family, as partners that sponsor new churches, we need to "raise" our family of new churches to have the healthy values we want them to have as mature churches someday. My wife and I have six children that we have reared to be responsible adults. We worked hard to teach them to be responsible, to have a strong work ethic, to be ready for the day they will be completely ready to live as adults who care for themselves and their families. We would feel like we had failed if somehow we reared children who thought a good strategy for living would be to rely on the government for welfare, or who could never leave our home because we had not prepared them well for a responsible adult life of living responsibly in society.

Partners Should Know Their Planters

Healthy organizational partnerships are really healthy relationships. If we are like a family, then we realize we are a rich tapestry of the way God has made us as individuals. If your church is going to partner with a planter or team, they need to be dealt with as the unique person or team they are in Christ. Every person has individual gifts, abilities, and passions. I have not used boilerplate templates of job descriptions when partnering with the planters we have sponsored. Every person and team is unique. Every church planting context is different. We take into consideration the lead planter's personality and the team's strengths and weaknesses. We try to discover their concerns and fears and address those early on in the process. We try to understand their expectations of the partnership and be crystal clear on these issues from the outset. Some planters' expectations are different from those in their team. We attempt to identify a shared group vision and then get everybody on the same page. Just like a dating relationship, this can take some time. Friendships can be made quickly, but they take time to grow and mature. As catalysts in our network, we believe the partnership is a relationship. Since we don't usually do salary funding, it changes the nature of the partnership. We are freed to be friends and Kingdom family without the encumbrances of financial issues getting in the way.

Planters Should Know Their Partners

Relationships with partners go in both directions. Occasionally I encounter a church planter filled with expectations of entitlement. The planter has the idea that the partner should be generous and sensitive to the planter's needs, but the planter or planting team is not aware of the hopes and needs of the partners. Organizational partners have reasons they get involved in church planting. Most of them are noble and Kingdom-minded. The wholehearted church planter carries the responsibility to be intentional in knowing the needs, hopes, desires, and expectations of the partners. This awareness is part of building a healthy relationship that leads to healthy partnerships.

Healthy alignment is a fruit of planters and partners knowing each other and being intentional in meeting those needs. It is important that there is agenda harmony and shared vision in healthy organizational relationships. A large part of that responsibility is shared by the planter and planting team. Time, trust, and openness in communication lead to a mutual admiration that is key to having healthy organizational relationships. Wholehearted church planters understand this and are very intentional in knowing the needs and expectations of their partners.

Tools for the Partnership

Several "tools" can be used to facilitate healthy organization partnerships. The first tool is a "**covenant**." I mentioned that I don't use boilerplate job descriptions. Whether they are for an employee of an organization, a volunteer in our agency, or a church planter partner, "covenants" are an excellent tool. I like to tailor the covenant to the individual. I like to write the agreement so that the other party to the covenant gets excited when first reading the covenant and becomes eager to live it out. I like to write the passions of the planter into the covenant, so the planter is jazzed to live it out. Covenants can give accountability, clarify expectations between both partners, and incorporate the unique gifts, abilities, and passions of the wholehearted planter or team. Covenants are negotiated in healthy relationships and mutually agreed upon. They are not "top down" documents, but are understandings between friends. This is the wholehearted climate in which I prefer to operate. Planters we have had covenants with through the years have said that they appreciate this kind of relationship better than other ways they have been related to in the past. Covenants are a wholehearted tool.

Networks

Another tool in our toolbox is the "network." This word is used and over-used, and means many different things in the church planting context. Some networks are very formal and require membership tied to expectations, and even membership fees. In 2002, we planted a church and named it "Ethne Church Network." When we credentialed our church with our denomination, they had many questions. Was it a church? Yes. Was it a network? Yes, at least that was the vision. We could only answer the questions humbly based on what it was and what we hoped it to be. The idea has evolved over ten years. We now have over twenty churches and other ministries connected to our network. Some of the initial concepts of the network were not practical and/or desired by the churches, but the network has value in creating relational encouragement, sourcing mentoring, and enabling some joint ministry and mission opportunities. One of the biggest encouragements has been through efforts to communicate prayer needs throughout the network. Praying for each other has been fruit bearing. We have had great successes—and some challenges—as we have journeyed to discover the best way to relate to each other. Still, organized properly, networks can be a wholehearted tool.

Mentoring

"Mentoring" is another term used to mean many different ideas. My first mentor was Jon Cook, my high school youth minister at church. Jon invested personal time and energy into me and discipled me. I know I am the person I am today in part because he helped me to walk a healthy path in that crucial stage of life. In 1996, Kenny Moore approached me and asked if he could "practice" this new skill he was being trained to do. Truth is, Kenny had been a mentor to many people before it was stylish to call it that. Nevertheless, since that time, Kenny has served as my mentor, providing one of the most life-giving relationships in my lifetime. We have been close friends for eighteen years, a big chunk of our lives. The last nine years we have been daily prayer partners. I have been a pastor where I have preached to hundreds of people on Sunday mornings, but I believe in a principle that is biblical and Christlike: *You make a bigger contribution to the Kingdom of God when you spend more time with fewer people.* It is countercultural to our ideas of "success" in ministry. I would challenge you to prayerfully ask God to give you a mentor, and to seek that person out as God directs. More specifically, I would challenge all wholehearted church planters to prayerfully ask God into whom He would like you to invest your life as a mentor. Prioritize this and carve out the time and energy in your life to make it happen. If you have children, this is a great place to start. Become a mentor and give intentional discipleship time to them. It is the simplest way to be obedient to the Great Commission: to make disciples. Mentoring is a great tool for wholehearted church planters.

Prayer Discipleship

Several years ago I traveled to the island of Borneo, on the Malaysian side, to visit the Iban[8] tribes. Mike Morgan, one of the pastors in our network, traveled with me. While there, we discovered a principle that we have used ever since, with God's help, with great results. The challenge was how to disciple some new believers when they had no curriculum in their language and no mature believer in their longhouse village. God gave me an idea that I have since developed and practiced and then taught in a variety of contexts since with great return on the investment.

A growing host of missionaries and missiologists perceive that "right belief" doesn't even mean someone is "saved," let alone is a disciple. Lots of people, especially in the West, could pass a test on right doctrine and yet have no fruit of transformation. After over a century of curriculum-based discipleship, as a whole Christians know much more than ever before, but have a weaker faith. If we don't use "curriculum," many have asked, "How then do you do evangelism and discipleship?" We take several steps:

1. we develop relationships with people;
2. we tell our story about how the Holy Spirit transformed us;
3. we talk about being a follower of Jesus;
4. we love people;
5. we help them;
6. we show them Jesus with skin on;
7. we talk of Scriptures as authoritative; and
8. we tell stories of faith.

None of this is new, but the newest "method" is to ask someone if we can pray with him/her everyday, in person or even on the cell phone, which is even becoming available in the entire global society, even the majority world. "Prayer Discipleship" is a commitment of two (or more) people to pray in community everyday, whether in person or by phone (or even e-mail), understanding that the prayer opens access to the transforming power of the Holy Spirit essential for our union with Christ and growth in who we are in Christ.

This "prayer discipleship" is not dependent on outside curriculum. Prayer discipleship uses the Holy Spirit's power in community in conjunction with Scripture to transform and grow followers of Jesus. It is contextual, cross-cultural, reproducible, and cheap. Its greatest asset to church planting and majority world missions is that it provides portal access to the power of the Holy Spirit. In the Great Commission, Jesus commanded us that as we go to make disciples of all the nations, and baptize and teach all his commandments, Jesus promises He will be with us until the end. "Prayer Discipleship" acknowledges that promise and becomes a new "curriculum" for making disciples where traditional methods and resources need to be supplemented.

Kenny and I decided that if this could work in Borneo, which it did, then it could work anywhere. We began to practice it in our own lives. It has been one of the richest parts of my daily life. We also began to use it as we mentored others in our network. Prayer discipleship is a great tool for wholehearted church planters, especially in the context of healthy organizational partnerships.

Relational Authority

Different kinds of authority operate in our lives. Positional authority comes from a formal position—one person has authority over another. A supervisor at work has authority over an employee. In the military, a general has authority over an enlisted man. Many organizations and even mission agencies are based on positional authority. This authority model is real, but a far more powerful form of authority functions in your everyday world. Relational authority is the powerful relationship that exists when people love and trust each other–respect and loyalty that are deep and rich exist between the two parties. If a supervisor demands an employee follow a directive, the employee will likely comply, but only out of an obligation to submit to authority. However, if a mentor or a prayer partner with whom we are in covenant suggests or advises a course of action, the mentee complies out of a deference that comes with love, respect, and trust. Out of the two examples, relational authority is much more life-giving, desired, and wholehearted.

Covenants, networks, and prayer discipleship are all excellent tools, but they are less effective in the context of positional authority. When two parties share relational authority, the authority becomes a deep and rich part of healthy organizational partnerships. We would encourage partners to be intentional in taking the time and energy to develop a relationship that makes genuine relational authority the normal way of relating to each other. This kind of love, respect, and trust is the wholehearted way to have healthy organizational partnerships. Experience shows most church planters would prefer to relate to partners this way.

Chapter 17

Loving Self Appropriately

ALLAN KARR

Loving Yourself?

In a Christian context that purports to value humility and to denigrate selfishness, this principle of appropriate self-love is sometimes hard to grasp. In my favorite church planting chapter of the Bible, Luke 10, Jesus is teaching His disciples. In this conversation, a lawyer asks Jesus, "Teacher, what shall I do to inherit eternal life?" (Lk. 10:25, NASB). Jesus replied with a question, asking the lawyer what was written in the Law, referring to the Law of Moses. The lawyer answered by quoting two verses; one was Deuteronomy 6:5 out of the Shema regarding loving God completely. The second passage he quoted was Leviticus 19:18b, which states, "…you shall love your neighbor *as yourself*" (NASB, emphasis added). Jesus affirms this answer by referencing Leviticus 18:5 and saying that if he does this, he will live. The lawyer then asks Jesus to clarify, so that he could be sure to follow the letter of the Law. He asks Jesus, "And who is my neighbor?" (Lk. 10:29, NASB). Jesus responds by telling the famous story that is often referred as the parable of the "Good Samaritan." We tend to focus, rightly so, on the principle of this parable of loving our neighbor. However, this principle is incomplete if the qualifying statement "as yourself" is ignored.

Another chapter of this book discusses love of God. Here we look at Jesus' command that we love self. Wholehearted church planters are engaged in loving themselves in a way that makes them better equipped and ready to love their neighbors, including all the people in their macro- and microcommunities.

Love of self is a crucial principle in understanding the story Jesus told. In defining "neighbor," Jesus told a story about a man who was trekking from Jerusalem to Jericho. Robbers mugged him, severely beat him up, stripped him of all his possessions, and left him for dead. Two "religious" guys ventured by and ignored him, not wanting to sully themselves with the problem. A third guy, technically a cultural enemy, came upon this injured stranger and felt compassion on him. He cleaned the victim's wounds, bandaged him up, put him on his animal, and carried him to an inn to receive further care. He stayed overnight with the injured man and then paid for his care and stated that he would return to check on him and pay any additional expenses.[1]

Jesus finished the story and then asked a question with an obvious answer, "Which of these three do you think proved to be a neighbor to the man who fell into robbers' hands?" (Lk. 10:36, NASB). The obvious answer pointed to the last guy, who showed him mercy. Then Jesus commanded, "Go and do the same" (Lk. 10:37b, NASB). We often, rightly so, focus on the "going" and "loving your neighbor" as important commands of Jesus to be obeyed. However, the power of the commands is subtly found in the qualifier to love your neighbor "*as yourself.*" This qualifier fulfills another principle in another of Jesus' great speeches– the "Sermon on the Mount."[2] There Jesus taught how God answers prayers: "So in everything, do to others *what you would have them do to you,* for this sums up the Law and the Prophets" (Mt. 7:12, emphasis added). The "Good Samaritan" felt compassion for the victim and helped him. His compassion was grounded in how he hoped someone would have treated him, even going the extra mile. Wholehearted people understand that to best fulfill Jesus' command to love our neighbors, we must first love ourselves appropriately.

Love Yourself in Appropriate Ways

Wholehearted church planters are kind, generous, compassionate, and self-sacrificial. These are attractive qualities as church planters minister to their macrocommunities and their microcommunities. However, a lifestyle absent of self-care is not conducive to long-term sustainable health and energy. Wholehearted people are intentionally kind to ourselves, not in a selfish way, but in a way that reflects the way that God loves us. If we look at ourselves the way God loves us, we are free to take intentional steps to care for ourselves the way our Father loves us, and to design a sustainable lifestyle for our personal health and the enjoyment of our ministry.

When I was an adolescent, generous and caring people in my church gave me a scholarship that made it possible for me to attend the Navigator youth ministry called *Eagle Lake Camp* outside of Colorado Springs.[3] The four-summer Eagle Lake experience became a milestone of formation in my spiritual life and character. There I learned an important principle of living a balanced life, illustrated by the life of Jesus as a young man.

The little we are told of Jesus' childhood is chronicled in Luke 2. The chapter tells the story of Jesus' birth, of His dedication at the Temple, of the prophecies Simeon and Anna spoke over Him, of His pilgrimage to Jerusalem when He was twelve, and of His amazing interaction with the teachers in the Temple. At the end of this chapter, one verse encapsulates Jesus' developmental years, rich with life principles: "And Jesus kept increasing in wisdom and stature, and in favor with God and men" (Lk. 2:52, NASB). This verse implies Jesus was growing in four areas of His life: emotional and intellectual maturity, physical health, spiritual closeness to God, and social relationships with people. The verse describes the balanced life Jesus modeled for us to live. It creates the foundational principle on which to design a life–wholehearted church planters love ourselves in appropriate and balanced ways.

Creating a Margin in Life

In our first book, Linda and I introduced the concept of "White Space" into the working vocabulary of church planting. The concept is illustrated by a page of a book; if every part of the page were completely filled, including the margins, the page would be not only hard to read but would leave no room to interject new ideas as notes in the margins. Maintaining white space in our lives allows us room to care for ourselves and to have room to help others, as the Good Samaritan helped a needy man he encountered on the road.

My prayer partner, Jim Misloski, introduced me to a similar concept in maintaining healthy margins in our lives. Jim occasionally speaks in my classes introducing this concept to the church planters we train. Jim illustrates the idea of intentionally creating margins in our lives from the maritime law of the *Plimsoll Mark*. The history of the *Plimsoll Mark* is tied to merchants overloading their ships in an attempt to maximize profits. In doing so, the safety of the ship and crew and cargo was compromised. Lloyds of London, a famous insurance company, had vested interest in seeing improvement in the safety of cargo vessels. Samuel Plimsoll, a nineteenth-century British merchant and shipping reformer, legislated placing a *Plimsoll Mark* on all shipping vessels. *The Plimsoll Mark* is "Waterlines to show the level the water should reach when the ship is properly loaded."[4] *The Plimsoll Mark* may be further explained:

> *Plimsoll line*, also called *Plimsoll mark*, official name international load line, internationally agreed-upon reference line marking the loading limit for cargo ships. At the instigation of one of its members, Samuel Plimsoll, a merchant and shipping reformer, the British Parliament, in the Merchant Shipping Act of 1875, provided for the marking of a load line on the hull of every cargo ship, indicating the maximum depth to which the ship could be safely loaded. Application of the law to foreign ships leaving British ports led to general adoption of load-line rules by maritime countries. An International Load Line was adopted by 54 nations in 1930, and in 1968 a new line, permitting a smaller freeboard (hull above waterline) for the new, larger ships, went into effect.[5]

The *Plimsoll Mark* looks like this, without the explanatory remarks.[6]

If a ship is loaded beyond the *Plimsoll Mark*, and so is sitting too low in the water, the ship has no margin of error if the ship encounters rough waters, a storm, or even comes across another vessel in need of rescue. If the load of the ship stays within the prescribed margins, fewer lives, ships, and cargo are lost.

The application to the lives of wholehearted people is obvious. If we load our "ship," our life, to the point that it is in danger of sinking even in calm waters, we are in definite danger should we encounter the inevitable storm. If we are so loaded that we cannot respond to an unplanned need of our neighbor: a family member, a team member, a friend, an acquaintance from the community, or even a stranger, we leave no margin for God to use us and bless us in His divine appointments. How sad would it be to see someone in need of rescue and you unable to help because in doing so you would sink your own ship? God wants us to have margins, whether defined as *White Space* or the principle of the *Plimsoll Mark.* These margins help us to have balanced lives and form the platform for loving ourselves appropriately.

Working in Teams

One popular strategy of church planting is called the "parachute drop." In this strategy, a target people group, usually identified as a geographic community, is identified. A church planter, often with his family, feels called to go to this place identified as needing a church.. The planter is often not indigenous to the field and is often an outsider to the culture. The family moves to the field, "parachuted in," using the analogy of a foreign battlefield being infiltrated by an invading army. The difference is that this family is usually alone, without any reinforcements. While using the "parachute drop" strategy has created many successful church plants, the experience usually involves a difficult and painful experience for the planting family. This strategy is not the most appropriate way for wholehearted planters to love their selves.

We are suggesting a much kinder and sustainable strategy. We would also argue it is a biblical model. In Luke 10:1, Jesus quite intentionally sent His disciples out in teams of two. Even if you go with your spouse, a biblical perspective is that, in marriage, the two become one. While going with a spouse is better than being alone, it is not the team strategy we are recommending as a more loving and sustainable model. We have observed over many years of church planting that a strategy of planting with a team is far more preferred than the "parachute drop," where the church planting family has to sink or swim by themselves.

Realistically, teams have their own challenges as well. Everyone on the team has their own expectations of the new church plant and their role in that new church. Before teams are deployed, they need to spend lots of time together. The best way to spend time together is praying and letting each person know the heart of the others. This also helps to clarify motives and let each person line his or her life up with the direction of the Holy Spirit for the new church. Additionally, team members need the time to develop trust in each other, in the lead planter, and in the common vision and direction of the new church. This cannot be adequately done in a few informational vision-casting meetings. Teams are intimate relationships, and team chemistry is only built by spending lots of time together, on and off the "field." If a new church can be planted by a team that has a healthy dynamic, that intimately trusts each other's gifts and motives, and that genuinely loves each other, the team–along with the Holy Spirit–has created a great environment to nurture wholehearted church planters who love themselves appropriately.

Be a Receiver

People called to serve others are often not very good at allowing others to serve them. Jesus encountered this when He took a towel and basin and started to wash the feet of His disciples. John 13 tells this important story about Jesus at the Passover feast just before He was arrested:

> Jesus knew that the Father had put him in complete charge of everything, that he came from God and was on his way back to God. So he got up from the supper table, set aside his robe, and put on an apron. Then he poured water into a basin and began to wash the feet of the disciples, drying them with his apron. When he got to Simon Peter, Peter said, "Master, *you* wash *my* feet?"
>
> Jesus answered, "You don't understand now what I am doing, but it will be clear enough to you later."
>
> Peter persisted, "You're not going to wash my feet–ever!"
>
> Jesus said, "If I don't wash you, you can't be part of what I am doing."[7]

Jesus was not concerned about the hygiene of Peter's body, but the holiness of his character.

I used to struggle with being a receiver of other people's generosity, even awkwardly arguing–until one day a loving parishioner said, "Pastor, please don't rob me of the blessing of doing this for you." You may think you are being humble by not wanting to be served or be the recipient of others' generosity. However, in part, accepting service is the economy of the Kingdom of God. He often prompts others to give generously to you as a blessing of encouragement. For example, God gives some people the gift of hospitality. They bless others in the Kingdom and, in doing so, the Father gives them an encouraging hug.[8]

In Luke 10 and Matthew 10, Jesus even teaches His disciples to take no provisions with them on their missionary journey:

> Jesus gave specific directions to His disciples that forced them to depend on others for their needs. Yet he made it clear that they were not to charge anyone for their services. In other words, no fee system for services rendered, rather they relied on the hospitality of those they ministered to and among. "Heal the sick, raise the dead, cleanse lepers, cast out demons. You receive without pay, give without pay." "Take no gold, nor silver, nor copper in your purses, no bag for your journey, nor two tunics, nor sandals, nor staff; for the laborer deserves his food." (Mt. 10:8–10)[9]

This passage teaches the disciples a crucial reliance on the providence of God, along with the parallel benefit of teaching the disciples to be gracious receivers of what He is providing. Being wholehearted church planters means we develop the capacity to give generously and serve kindly when prompted, but also to receive graciously when God prompts others to show love to us. Embrace such moments as a hug from the loving Father and as a reminder of the richness of the loving relationships with which He has surrounded you.

Another aspect of being a receiver is in the context of fundraising. My former student, traveling companion, and good friend Mike Morgan has been my mentor in this area of ministry. He has modeled effective fundraising in a way that is Kingdom-minded and wholehearted both for a parachurch ministry and as a church planter in our network.[10] Mike has taught me that fundraising is biblical. In fact, the whole chapter of 2 Corinthians 9 is about the biblical principles of raising funds for ministry. Mike has taught many people to raise funds, but most church planters usually do not heed his training, as it requires a focus of time and energy for a season of life. Most planters choose not to make this the priority it needs to be to properly raise support. Mike and Kate Morgan are my heroes, as they are modeling to the Kingdom how to be gracious receivers of God's provision. This quality is important for wholehearted planters to love themselves appropriately.

Keep the "Sabbath"

Several years ago, God's Spirit prompted me to learn more about the Sabbath. I learned that it is a divisive issue among God's people. Some Christian's argue very adamantly that the Sabbath and the laws connected with it should be completely ignored. They have made an entire case against following the Sabbath, using a barrage of scripture quoted to support their case. Other believers, just as adamant, make a strong case for following the Sabbath, even to the letter of the law, and give scriptural evidence to support their views. I would suggest a more balanced approach that avoids the extremes of either position.

You can honor the Sabbath principle God established in creation while also honoring the grace Jesus introduced to us, freeing us from the bondage of legalities.

At the time of creation, God established a rhythm of expending energy and recuperating energy. God created for six days and then He rested, not so much because He was tired, but to establish for all of creation, from human beings to even the land, that this divine rhythm of life is part of a comprehensive plan. The Sabbath principle is more than a physical issue of getting tired and then being rested. God holistically tied in a spiritual issue as well. Since humans are not God, we need an intentional time to regularly focus on Him so we can recharge our spiritual batteries and gain strength from the One who gives it to us.

Most Christians still value the "Ten Commandments" from Exodus 20 as important foundational values upon which to build a life that gives glory to God. Exodus 20:8–11 says, "Observe the Sabbath day, to keep it holy…,"[11] and then spends the rest of the passage explaining that principle. The Israelites wanted to make sure they kept the Sabbath "holy," and so developed a whole set of traditional rules to follow to verify they were keeping the command.

When Jesus came to earth, He began to challenge the traditions of the Sabbath, the rules established to measure obedience to this principle. New Testament writers speak often on the issue, trying to reestablish the principle in the context of the grace of the gospel of the Kingdom of God. In the generations since, Christians have struggled to find unity in what is a principle and what is an extra-biblical tradition. In my tradition of faith, Sunday was set apart as "The Lord's Day."[12] It was often used as a premise to coerce church members to attend Sunday worship services as a "day of rest." Yet for many years I have served the local church and was the pastor of churches with a full set of programs. Sunday quickly became my busiest day of the week. At the end of a Sunday, I was very tired. There was no rest involved on that day for me or for the hundreds of laity who were not even vocational ministers, but were simply participants and leaders in the programs of the day. We finished our day of "rest" exhausted. Some pastors I know take Monday off to recuperate from the energy expended on Sunday, yet the nonvocational lay leaders usually had to get up on Monday and go to work. Practically speaking, in that context we are not following the principle of the Sabbath, and we are certainly not "loving ourselves appropriately."

From this reality I began a quest to discover a practical way to honor the Sabbath, worship God, gather to worship collectively with my church community, and still love my neighbor as myself in a holistically spiritually healthy way. I value the Bible as my authoritative instructions for living, so it must contain some guidance to help in this issue. In Matthew 12:12, Jesus teaches that the Sabbath is a day to show kindness to people, to show mercy rather than religiosity, as He also taught in Matthew 12:7. The other three Gospels are consistent in their treatment of the Sabbath:

> In both Mark and Luke, Christ is cited as saying the same thing by means of a rhetorical question, precisely that on the Sabbath it is lawful "to do good" and "to save" (Mark 3:4; Luke 6:9). In Luke, Christ is reported as saying that the Sabbath is the day to loose human beings from physical and spiritual bonds (Luke 13:12, 16). In John, Christ invites His followers to share on the Sabbath in the divine redemptive activity (John 9:4; 5:17; 7:22–23). Therefore, the unanimous view of the Gospels is that Christ presented the Sabbath as a time to serve God especially by rendering loving service to human needs.[13]

I began to ponder if part of the way to honor the principle of the Sabbath was tied to the command not only to love God with all of our holistic beings but also to love our neighbors as ourselves. What if spiritual rest and recuperating energy included a combination of worship of the Father and then giving of our resources (physical, emotional, financial, et al.) to love and serve other people in need?

> The positive humanitarian understanding of Sabbathkeeping is rooted in Christ's fulfillment of the redemptive typology of the Sabbath, which we found brought out in the Gospels in several ways. Viewing the rest and redemption typified by the Old Testament Sabbath as realized by Christ's redemptive mission, New Testament believers regarded Sabbathkeeping as a day to celebrate and experience the Messianic redemption-rest by showing "mercy" and doing "good" to those in need. What this means to us Christians today is that on and through the Sabbath we celebrate Christ's creative and redemptive accomplishments by acting redemptively toward others.[14]

This seems like a key ingredient to a more balanced approach to keeping the Sabbath. No one formula expresses this for everyone. My family and faith community practice this principle by keeping a rhythm of life with appropriate rest. We are committed to keep our personal time with God, but very intentional to gather regularly with other believers to worship God together and encourage one another.[15] This spiritual health is only possible when recognized as a rhythm, like breathing. We breathe in to get more oxygen, and we exhale as part of the rhythm of life that God has designed to work with all living systems. For us, keeping the Sabbath includes "breathing out" by serving others. We view our corporate worship as a way to be strengthened to leave the gathering and go live the values in our everyday lives, as light and salt (Mt. 5:13–16) and as humanitarians to the "orphans and widows" (Jas. 1:27). We found that in living life this way, we were recharging our batteries. We cannot find words to describe how energizing it is to be hugged by an orphan who genuinely loves you.[16] There is no way to describe the emotional lift when your kindness to the marginalized of life bears spiritual fruit in the Kingdom. Connecting to this divine rhythm is part of the way we love ourselves appropriately. We honor the divine principle of Sabbath. We avoid burnout. We live a holistically sustainable life.

Set Boundaries

In an earlier chapter, I told you about the twelve challenges that my wife Kathy presented to planters. One of those challenges dealt with the busyness of the home of the church planting family. Remember what Kathy said in her challenges. Still more needs to be said on this issue in thinking about how to love ourselves appropriately. Wholehearted church planters can have more sustainable and healthier ministries if they learn to appropriately set boundaries in their lives and ministries.

Date Nights. Early in our first church plant, Kathy and I only had three children. Even finding a "cheap" babysitter was very expensive for our frugal church planting income and budget. The cost of our childcare could easily far surpass the cost of the rest of a date together for an evening. Our sponsoring church recognized this need, and on several occasions they either provided volunteers to help with our children or provided the funds specifically for the babysitter so Kathy and I could have an occasional date. We had people who cared for us in this special way.[17]

Spending intentional time together is crucial for the health of your marriage. This advice is not only for church planters, but the need for a date night is especially true in this season of your life. Often your financial budget does not allow for even only moderately expensive dates, such as dinner and a movie. However, you can find creative ways to date frugally. Kathy and I started our courtship from our first date using coupons to restaurants and going to dollar movies. (We were in seminary at the time.)

You can take walks or hikes, or go to a coffee shop for a long conversation. (Make a rule to talk about other things than "church.") Even just doing some family shopping without small children in tow is redemptive and rejuvenating to your spirit, as you can reconnect and talk intimately. Wholehearted people love themselves by caring for their marriage relationships.

"Days off." In the first season of a church plant, lives can be very busy. You often give more than you receive, so it can be draining. In ministry, people will take as much time as you give them. Church plants inevitably attract some of the most needy and high maintenance people. The church planting team should encourage or even insist on an agreement for days off and family time *away* from the house and office. Often, if you are trying to take a day off, people will still find you at home. Wholehearted church planters are generous with their time and will lose the opportunity for a much-needed break. Often, Kathy and I will load up our children and drive away from our own community and go get ice cream cones or even just do family shopping. The emotional benefits of the change in routine are bountiful. Even if it is only for small breaks or for a few hours here and there, try to do some things that are totally nonchurch-related so that you are not doing church 24/7, as attractional models often seem to require.[18]

Vacations and Retreats. We encourage you to take advantage of opportunities to get away for longer periods of time when possible. Pray for opportunities and take them when they come, even if you don't feel you need it. We were blessed to have an annual denominational retreat for church planters, which in Colorado was always in a retreat setting. We always appreciated this gift from our partners. We also had a sponsoring church that provided opportunities to get away, since they were aware that we were on a limited budget that often did not include discretionary income for vacations. We had Christian families who had second homes in the mountains offer us the use for a weekend or even longer, and we have good memories of the vacations that were provided for our family. Mission conferences were often a time of refreshment for us. We also used time off for visits to our families in other states, which, besides the relational benefits, were often affordable ways to get away for needed rest.

For the long-term health of the planter, the planting family, and the church, the wholehearted church planter needs to set boundaries for his or her time and home. Date nights, days off, retreats, and vacations are important priorities to include in these boundaries. Wholehearted church planters learn to set healthy boundaries in a holistic life of ministry.

Attention to Physical Health. Living a balanced and healthy life includes giving attention to diet, exercise, and proper rest. When you are younger you might not sense the urgency of this. However I can attest from experience that when you move into a middle-aged season of life it is much harder to fix a health problem than it would be to maintain physical health all through your life. My mentor constantly encouraged me and held me accountable in this area of my life. As our children got older, healthy lifestyles were a part of their values and have become a way we spend family time together. It is a key way to love yourself appropriately.

Learning to Ask for Help. Church planters in dominant culture America are often wired in such a way that they are entrepreneurial, hard working, and self-reliant. Often we find personal value and form our own self-identities around these characteristics. These can be very positive qualities, but not if we rely on these qualities as our strategy for living rather than on who were are in Christ. Although much of our culture looks at these qualities as positive, such self-reliance is just what the apostle Paul refers to as "flesh." As positive as these qualities can be, people who are wired this way have a very difficult time asking others for help. Asking others for help is often viewed as a weakness, yet the hard-working missionary church planter Paul frequently asked people for help. It was even key to his relationships.

A key reality in church planting is that the church planting team cannot do everything in a church plant by themselves, nor should they. It is not even biblical. Romans 12:4–5 states, "For just as we have many members in one body and all the members do not have the same function, so we, who are many, are one body in Christ, and individually members of one another" (NASB). Other people are gifted. God created them to be active in the Body, the church, as well. Asking for help communicates that you value others' strengths and that you are humble enough to know you cannot do everything. Asking others for help also spreads out the blessings of serving God and lets others develop their ministry with on-the-job training. Asking for help also inspires others that you have confidence in them. Learning to ask for help taps into important ecclesiological and missiological principles about the church, but it also is an important ingredient in loving yourself appropriately. It reflects and reveals your wholeheartedness.

Conclusion

All this focusing on how to love self appropriately naturally implies that you could love yourself inappropriately. The world is full of ways through which people try to give themselves pleasure that do not honor God. The wisdom literature is full of warnings about inappropriate ways to love yourself. In our self-centered culture, Christians are wary of ideas that put a focus on the self and not on God. Heeding all these warnings is prudent. However, God loves us and wants us to love ourselves in a way that honors His love for us. In loving ourselves appropriately, wholehearted church planters express the holistic love of God and are poised to redemptively love their neighbors.

Chapter 18

Living a Whole Way of Life

LINDA BERGQUIST

*Before you know it, a sense of God's wholeness, everything coming together
for good, will come and settle you down.* –PHILIPPIANS 4:7, *THE MESSAGE*

Philosopher/teacher/author Dallas Willard pondered, "[F]aith today is
treated as something that only should make us different, not that actually
does make us different."[1] Loving God wholeheartedly actually *does* make
us different. It changes the things about which we are passionate, the direction and intensity of our prayers, and the scope of our knowledge and
wisdom. Loving God wholeheartedly heals our brokenness, transforms
our characters, and challenges our hopes and our aspirations. We think
more wholly and act more wholly because of Him. It is about who or what
is at the center of our lives.

The apostle Paul often admitted his own imperfections. He acknowledged his weaknesses, considered himself as the least of the apostles, and
conceded that he, himself, was not blameless. In the book of Philippians
he wrote, "Brothers and sisters, I do not consider myself yet to have taken
hold of it. But one thing I do: Forgetting what is behind and straining toward what is ahead, I press on toward the goal to win the prize for which
God has called me heavenward in Christ" (Phil. 3:13–14). Paul was not
perfect, but he was focused. He lived His life wholly around Jesus. Yet,
even as this greatest church planter in history struggled with his own sin,
so do church planters today.

Wholeness Made Possible

In their paradigm-shifting book, *The Missional Church in Perspective*, Craig
Van Gelder and Dwight Zscheile note, "Missional church is, on a deep
level, about theological imagination–a different way to see and experience life in the church and the world.[2] What if our theological imagination
propelled us towards an appreciation of God's wholeness that helped us
know and worship God more wholly? "God is whole, fully integrated,

unbroken, complete and holy. His patterns are to complete, restore; to reconcile all things to Himself; and to unite all things in Christ."[3] If these things are true about the nature of God, what can be deduced about the potential for all of those who are called by His name and about their capacity to love others in His name?

Living with Christ at the Center

Many people, including Linda and Allan, have written about centered groups in relationship to how Christians fellowship with one another. Centered groups form around a common central idea, goal, issue, vision, or guiding principle. Members agree to travel in the same direction around that center. A centered *life* is similar. In this case, an individual makes a decision to anchor his or her self to some primary focal point. From that point on, that person's life is committed to traveling in a direction around this center. A wholehearted life is not about a destination, but a direction; it not so much a goal as it is the result of living out a life that is centered in Christ. Linda and Allan present this chapter not because we have "arrived," but because we have committed to the journey and because, one small step at a time, we sense that God is changing us, too.

Walking in the Way of Wholeness

We Must Acknowledge That God Alone Is Whole, and We Are Not

Twelve-step recovery programs begin with an admission of powerlessness. Addicts who enter these programs are required to admit that they are broken and cannot transform their lives by themselves. They make individual decisions to turn their broken lives over to God, as best as they know Him. This act of humility is the beginning of the journey to wholeness, as needy persons discover that not only are they *not* whole, but they are not even able to see the whole. God is whole because He is holy, and He is holy because He is whole. These statements are both true at once. He has also called His people to holiness: "But just as he who called you is holy, so be holy in all you do; for it is written: 'Be holy, because I am holy'" (1 Pet. 1:15–16).

The words *whole, holy, holistic,* and *health* are derived from the same Anglo-Saxon root word *hal.* In Hebrew, the word is *shalem,* meaning balanced, complete, or whole. This family of words shows up in diverse fields, such as in theoretical physicist David Bohm's book *Wholeness and the Implicate Order,* in the values system of the holistic health movement, in the architectural studies of Christopher Alexander, in Swiss psychiatrist Carl Jung's theories of human development, in systems thinking, and in various education theories.

Human beings, it seems, have a longing for wholeness. It is critical to recognize, however, that only in Christ is real wholeness possible. He is the vine, and we are merely branches (Jn. 15:5). "He was beaten so we could be whole. / He was whipped so we could be healed" (Isa. 53:5, NLT). When Jesus saves us from our sins, the path towards wholeness begins, but the spiritual battle does not stop there. The apostle Paul describes the raging inner battle and how, in the end, Jesus prevails:

> So I find this law at work: Although I want to do good, evil is right there with me. For in my inner being I delight in God's law; but I see another law at work in me, waging war against the law of my mind and making me a prisoner of the law of sin at work within me. What a wretched man I am! Who will rescue me from this body that is subject to death? Thanks be to God, who delivers me through Jesus Christ our Lord. (Rom. 7:21–25)

To Live Wholly, We Must Guard Our Hearts

The writer of Proverbs warned, "Above all else, guard your heart, for it is the wellspring of life" (Prov. 4:23). While this pertains to all spheres of life, in our experience, three key areas seem especially pertinent to church planters—sexual purity, pride, and money.

SEXUAL PURITY

When King David commissioned his son Solomon as the next leader and the builder of the Temple, he commended him in front of all of Israel's officials, saying, "And you, my son Solomon, acknowledge the God of your father, and serve him with wholehearted devotion and with a willing mind, for the LORD searches every heart and understands every desire and every thought. If you seek him, he will be found by you; but if you forsake him, he will reject you forever" (1 Chr. 28:9).

It is not clear in Scripture at what point Solomon first began collecting women for his own use, but eventually he amassed seven hundred wives and three hundred concubines. Many were foreign women who did not worship the God of Israel. Solomon not only allowed them to worship their foreign gods, but he also built places of worship for them. As he became old, Solomon began to follow those other gods. God became angry with him and punished him (1 Kings 11). This all happened to Solomon, once named the wisest man on earth, and it can happen to church planters today, too. Most church planters do not have staff or regular office space that can serve as "safe space" for cross-gender meetings. One possible solution to this problem is that partnering churches can provide such spaces. Both married and single planters must set boundaries before the need arises. Another helpful idea is for them to find accountability partners in order to protect themselves from sexually explicit materials, including Internet sources. Church planters need prayer from their entire support system that God will protect their hearts in this critical area.

PRIDE

Good church planters sometimes strain their relationships and undermine their effectiveness because they become overly impressed with their own selves. In the name of hard work and wise time investment, they become less and less available to people that they do not find particularly useful to their goals. Their egos become inflated to the extent that they forget how to cry with those who cry and how to get excited about the smaller successes of others. It is difficult to truly love others and to love God when one is self-centered or prideful. Another danger of pride is that some individuals set themselves up as teachers of others too quickly, often at the expense of their own openness to learning new things. They position themselves as "answer people" instead of lead navigators.[4] The whole point of this book is that God is more interested in our characters than in our accomplishments. Jeremiah 9:24 warns, "[B]ut let the one who boasts boast about this: / that they have the understanding to know me, / that I am the LORD."[5]

MONEY

Finally, church planters must guard their hearts in matters pertaining to money. "What money?" those who are planters may ask. Church planters, whether they are bi-vocational or funded by people and organizations, are almost always stretched to live by faith. That can be really tough and even painful, but "The LORD is [your] shepherd; [you] shall not want" (Ps. 23:1, NASB). It is not easy to, like Paul, learn "...to be content, whatever the circumstances may be...[to] know now how to live when things are difficult and...when things are prosperous (Phil. 4:11–13). God will not stop caring about the needs of church planters. "I have been young and now I am old, yet I have not seen the righteous forsaken or his descendants begging bread" (Ps. 37:25, NASB).

Scripture pinpoints a problem with not trusting God to meet our needs: "But the worries of the world, and the deceitfulness of riches, and the desires for other things enter in and choke the word, and it becomes unfruitful" (Mk. 4:19, NASB). Partner churches and denominational leaders who are reading this, how can you help to shoulder some of the concern church planters have about finances? "Now to Him who is able to do far more abundantly beyond all that we ask or think, according to the power that works within us" (Eph. 3:20, NASB).

Another concern about finances is that church planters sometimes choose the harvest field in which they plant at least partially based on money considerations. Both poor neighborhoods and wealthy ones are neglected. Poor neighborhoods are neglected for reasons such as, "I don't want to raise a family there," or, "This neighborhood will never produce a self-supporting church that can pay me a full-time salary." Wealthy neighborhoods are neglected because residents are perceived as too difficult to reach or because "I could never afford to live there." These kinds of excuses are prudent, but spiritual wisdom should always precede earthly wisdom. Is God really telling church planters to only start churches among the middle class?

We Must Observe Wholeness in Our Work

People with type A, driven personalities score high on assessments that measure church planters for "intrinsic motivation." It would be easy to simply note that wholehearted people are driven by Kingdom goals and work hard to produce Kingdom fruit. These can be good things, but sometimes zealousness detracts from a church planter's devotion to God and to family. Wholeheartedness regarding the work of church planting is actually a different thing. It is more about how we approach our work, how we include or disenfranchise others, how our values are embedded in our work, and how we incorporate work into our ways of life. Nobody frames the concept better than Christian ecologist/author Wendell Berry:

> As the connections have been broken by the fragmentation and isolation of work, they can be restored by restoring the wholeness of work. There is work that is isolating, harsh, destructive, specialized or trivialized into meaninglessness. And there is work that is restorative, convivial, dignified and dignifying, and pleasing. Good work is not just the maintenance of connections—as one is now said to work "for a living" or "to support a family"—but the enactment of connections. It is living, and a way of living; it is not support for a family in the sense of an exterior brace or prop, but is one of the forms and acts of love.[6]

Practicing Wholeness in Community

A decision to fully commit to any center, such as mentioned earlier in this chapter, may be equated with some kind of a conversion experience, religious or not. For example, a drug addict whose way of life has been oriented around scoring a fix may decide to re-align life around staying drug-free, or an alcoholic may choose sobriety. The twelve-step process of Alcoholics Anonymous and its copycat addiction recovery program help people manage their lives around a new way of ordering their realities. Individuals make the big decision, but they play out that decision in the context of groups and mentors who hold one another accountable. In the same way, Christians who choose to live their lives around the Great Commandment, with Jesus in the center, do so best to the extent that they participate in community.

How will the church plant practice real community, call one another to a higher way, and live together around the Commandment? Practicing community helps us to see things in more whole ways. Here are some thoughts about what it takes. Note that these are relational practices.

Wholehearted Christians Practice Not Judging Others

Jesus' command to not judge (Mt. 7:1) is difficult to keep. It is a temptation that humans face many times each day, whether we verbalize it or not. This man speaks too loudly (maybe he is hard of hearing); that woman drives like she just got her license (maybe she did); this woman is walking too slowly (a knee injury?); that person reads like a first grader (severe dyslexia?). We posture ourselves as if we know the whole, but we do not. Judging others is a symptom of a greater problem in that it shows a lack of humility and a lack of love. Nobody can stop judging just by deciding to obey Jesus' command. It takes asking God to transform our persons and to give us humble hearts that submit to one another in love. We must realize that we need God and we need each other to find our way towards wholeness.

Wholehearted Christians Practice Treating Others More Highly Than They Treat Themselves

Why do so many people choose to compete with one another instead of complete one another? Why do we feel the need to prove that we are better, smarter, or richer? Why must we be the most fiscally and physically fit? Humility is not part of human nature, but it is the nature of Christ. Scripture says that Jesus, knowing God had given Him all authority and all power, wrapped a towel around His waist and began washing His disciples' feet (Jn. 13:3–5). Jesus, fully aware of who He was, lowered His body to the ground and took the posture of a servant. As the Father sent Jesus, so Jesus sends ordinary and extraordinary church planters, calling them to serve rather than to be served.

Wholehearted Christians Identify with the Poor

The devout young ruler had everything he wanted except eternal life, the one thing his money could not buy him. He was a good man who had faithfully tried to keep the Ten Commandments, but Jesus told this young man to be *telios* (complete/mature–translated as "perfect" in the KJV). For him, that meant selling everything he owned and giving the money to the poor. In other words, to be fully whole and complete, he needed not only to abandon his love of material things, but he also needed for the poor to receive what he had to give (Mk. 10:21–22). The man came to Christ wanting to receive eternal life, but only the *whole* gospel is good news, not just the part about eternal life. Richard Stearns writes prophetically, "God is concerned about the spiritual, physical, and social dimensions of our beings. This whole gospel is truly good news for the poor, and it is the foundation for a social revolution that has the power to change the world."[7]

What if the scenario were different and this rich man had followed Jesus' command to sell his belongings and give the money to the poor?

He had just been invited to join a community of homeless disciples who traveled with Jesus. If that had happened, he would have learned to completely identify with the poor since he would have become poor too. In another instance, Jesus sent out seventy-two people, two by two, to share the gospel. He told them not to take anything with them—not a purse, a bag, or even sandals. He also told them to eat and drink the food they were offered. They were utterly dependent on other people for their subsistence. This was the life into which Jesus invited the rich young ruler: a life of poverty, humility, and dependence that would somehow make him more complete and more whole—more wholehearted. How will you learn to identify with the poor, and how will you lead others to identify with them, too?

Concluding Words

Dear sisters, dear brothers: Let us pray for one another that we may ourselves be more wholehearted in our devotion and in the work to which the Father has called us. May the disciples you reproduce and the churches you start be a sweet-smelling offering in honor of our Lord. "Now may the God of peace make you holy in every way, and may your whole spirit and soul and body be kept blameless until our Lord Jesus Christ comes again" (1 Thess. 5:23, NLT). –LINDA AND ALLAN

Notes

Preface

1. Saint Augustine, *Confessions*, trans. Henry Chadwick, Oxford World's Classics (New York: Oxford Univ. Press, 2009), 397:29.

Chapter 1: Wholehearted Relationship with the Father

1. St. Patrick, from *The Confession of Saint Patrick, Book of Armagh* 450 A.D., line 16, http://www.ancienttexts.org/library/celtic/ctexts/p01.html

2. Ibid., line 15.

3. A. W. Tozer, "For Pastors Only," *Alliance Weekly* (May 6, 1950).

4. Brother Lawrence and F. Laubach, *The Practice of the Presence of God* (Sargent, Ga.: SeedSowers, 1973), 85.

5. Richard J. Krejcir, *Statistics on Pastors: What Is Going on with the Pastors in America?* (blog on site of the Francis Schaeffer Institute), http://www.intothyword.org/apps/articles/default.asp?articleid=36562.

6. Eugene Peterson, *Working the Angles: The Shape of Pastoral Integrity* (Grand Rapids: 1987), 2.

7. John MacArthur, *Ashamed of the Gospel: When the Church Becomes Like the World*, 3rd ed. (Wheaton, Ill.: Crossway Books, 2010), 72.

8. Attributed to Einstein.

9. Rick Warren (Radicalis Conference, Saddleback Church, Lake Forrest, Calif., Feb. 22–25, 2011).

Chapter 2: To Love a Greathearted God

1. See also Num. 14:18; Ps. 103:8; Neh. 9:17; Nah. 1:3.

2. Chip Ingram, *Good to Great in God's Eyes: 10 Practices Great Christians Have in Common* (Grand Rapids: Baker Books, 2007).

3. See Neil Cole's book *Cultivating a Life for God: Multiplying Disciples Through Life Transformation Groups* (Carol Stream, Ill.:ChurchSmart Resources, 1999).

Chapter 3: Knowing and Following Jesus with Whole Heart

1. Per my mentor and Greek scholar, Kenny Moore, in Matthew 28:19 the Greek word πορευθέντες (poreuthentes) is a 1st Aorist passive participle, nominative, plural, masculine. "Aorist" means it is a one point in time action without regard for the amount of time taken to accomplish the action. A "Passive" participle means the subject is the recipient of the action, i.e. the subject of the sentence is being acted upon (most often it is interpreted as God doing the acting upon). Kenny's suggested interpretation of this one word: "As you are going in my empowerment, start what you have not been doing and don't ever stop..." (Emailed document 2/20/2012).

2. Per Kenny Moore, the Greek verb μαθητεύσατε (*matheteusate*) is 1st Aorist, active, imperative, 2nd person plural. Aorist is as mentioned in the previous note,

and "active" indicates the subject is the performer of the action of the verb. "Imperative" is a command or instruction given to the hearer, often charging the hearer to carry out or perform a certain action. Kenny's suggested interpretation of the first phrase of Matthew 28:19 is, "As you are going in my empowerment, start what you have not been doing and don't ever stop. I am commanding you (instructing you) to be about the activity of making disciples…" (e-mail from 2/20/2012).

3. This is described by Jesus to Nicodemus in John 3:3–7. Jesus tells him, "You must be born again" (Jn. 3:7).

4. Per Kenny Moore, the Greek verb βαπτίζοντες (*baptizontes*) is present tense, active participle, nominative, plural, masculine. Present tense usually denotes a continuous kind of action, an action in progress or even a state of persistence (e-mail from 2/20/2012).

5. Per Kenny Moore, in Matthew 28:20, the Greek verb διδάσκοντες (*didaskontes*) is present tense, active participle nominative, plural, masculine. Kenny suggests an accurate interpretation would be, "*continuously* baptizing them in the name of the Father and of the Son and of the Holy Spirit, and *continuously* teaching them…" (e-mail from 2/12/2012).

6. John 14:15.

Chapter 4: Knowing God's Spirit

1. Roland Allen, *The Ministry of the Spirit: Selected Writings*, ed. David M. Paton (1960; reprinted Cambridge, U.K.: Lutterworth Press, 2011).

2. Ibid., 21.

3. All about Philosophy, "Deism-Enlightened Emptiness," http://www.allaboutphilisophy.org/deism.htm, accessed 3/2/2012.

Chapter 5: Response of Worship and Work

1. Quoted portions from Deuteronomy 6:5 and Leviticus 19:18.

2. Kenny Moore, Duane Arledge, and Larry Loser.

3. This is a tagline that my mentor Kenny Moore includes in the signature section of every e-mail he sends out. The idea is not original, but the specific wording is his.

Chapter 6: Knowing a People and Their Place

1. Virgil, *The Georgics*, trans. Smith Palmer Bovie (Chicago: The University of Chicago Press, 1966), 5.

2. Neil Gaiman, "The Kindly Ones," *The Sandman*, vol. 9 (New York: Vertigo, 1996), 115.

3. See the chart layers of cultural exegesis on the last page of this chapter.

4. See the chapter 1 description in this book of Caleb as a wholehearted man, based on this same story from Numbers.

5. Antoine de Saint-Exupéry. *The Little Prince* (New York: Brace, 1943), 202.

6. From http://quickfacts.census.gov/qfd/index.html.

7. From www.mla.org.

8. From http://www.diversitycentral.com.

9. From http://www.google.com/alerts.

10. From http://familypedia.wikia.com/wiki/List_of_most_common_surname.

11. From http://www.thearda.com.

12. See http://www.arcgis.com/home/webmap/viewer.html?webmap=843f3c 1004184ba9bffc0d7505573760&extent=-122.5567,37.7165,-122.3354,37.811

13. C. Clayman and M. Lee, *ethNYcity: The Nations, Tongues, and Faiths of Metropolitan New York* (New York: Metro New York Baptist Association and Baptist State Convention of North Carolina, 2010).

14. See http://www.topsite.com/goto/zipskinny.com.

Chapter 7: Knowing Near and Far People

1. Tokunboh Adeyemo, *African Bible Commentary* (Nairobi, Kenya: WordAlive Publishers, 2006), 1425.

2. "The Far and the Near" was published first in *Cosmopolitan* magazine in 1935 and reprinted in Thomas Wolfe's book of collected stories, *From Death to Morning* (New York: C. Scribner's Sons, 1935).

3. Felicity Dale, *An Army of Ordinary People: Stories of Real-Life Men and Women Simply Being the Church* (Carol Stream, Ill.: BarnaBooks, 2010).

Chapter 8: Three Tenses of Knowing a Community

1. See Linda Bergquist and Allan Karr, *Church Turned Inside Out: A Guide for Designers, Refiners and Re-Aligners* (San Francisco: Jossey-Bass, 2010), 3.

2. Roger Martin, as quoted in Bill Breen, "The Business of Design," *Fast Company Magazine* (April 1, 2005), http://www.fastcompany.com/magazine/93/design.html. For more on this topic see Roger L. Martin, *The Design of Business: Why Design Thinking Is the Next Competitive Advantage* (Boston: Harvard Business School Press, 2009).

3. http://travel.nytimes.com/2012/01/08/travel/45-places-to-go-in-2012.html?page wanted=all (January 8, 2012).

4. Wes Jackson, *Becoming Native to This Place* (Lexington: University of Kentucky Press, 1994), 15.

5. "A Mourning City Asks Why," *The San Francisco Examiner*, November 28, 1978.

Chapter 9: Team Perspective on Knowing

1. Years later, Kathy observed that we were a team planting the church, but in the later institutional recollection of it, people only seemed to talk about the "church that Allan planted…" I will affirm that Kathy worked side-by-side and back-to-back with me at all times. It is arguable that she even worked harder than I did when you consider the behind-the-scenes tasks of hospitality and organization that she performed. Clearly, our culture needs to be corrected to acknowledge the hard work of everyone involved in a church plant, not just the lead planter.

2. "Bi-vocational" means several things in church culture. It can mean that the pastor/planter earns some income from the church, but most often the entire income for the person or family comes from secular employment outside the church plant. In this case the second "vocation" is the volunteer calling to plant the church.

3. John 19:30.

4. James 3:13–18; Galatians 5:3–5, 13–15.

5. Ecclesiastes 3:1–2 (NASB).

6. It is commonly assumed that this phrase is a quote from the Bible. In actuality it is not. It is a popularized phrase to sum up the idea from Ecclesiastes that there is a time for everything, and then it "passes."

Chapter 10: Loving a Microcommunity

1. Linda Bergquist and Allan Karr, *Church Turned Inside Out: A Guide for Designers, Refiners and Re-Aligners* (San Francisco: Jossey-Bass, 2010), 35--36.

2. Gary Chapman, *The Five Love Languages: How to Express Heartfelt Commitment to Your Mate* (Chicago: Northfield Publishing, 2010).

Chapter 11: Loving a People

1. At that time Mae La Camp, close to Mae Sot, was one of seven official UNHCR refugee camps located all along the Burma border in Thailand where hundreds of thousands of refugees, not all Karen, were living indefinitely.

2. As listed in Galatians 5:22–23.

3. Ethne Global Services. See http://www.ethneglobalservices.org/whoweare.html.

4. The first book Linda and I co-wrote was on this design process. Linda Bergquist and Allan Karr, *Church Turned Inside Out: A Guide for Designers, Refiners and Re-Aligners* (San Francisco: Jossey-Bass, 2010).

5. From *12 Challenges for the Spouses on a Church Planting Team.* From "1.Verify a Strong Sense of Call." This is an unpublished document but was presented in several church planting training venues by Kathy Karr.

Chapter 12: Discovering Your Missional Love Language

1. Gary Chapman, *The Five Love Languages: How to Express Heartfelt Commitment to Your Mate* (Chicago: Northfield Publishing, 1992).

2. Dorothy Bass, *Receiving the Day* (San Francisco: Jossey-Bass, 2000), 3.

3. New church baby showers provide the opportunity for partnering churches to involve every church member in the process of giving. The church plants present a list of needs, and members bring Bibles, coffeemakers, crayons, portable cribs, etc.

4. Reggie McNeal, *Missional Renaissance: Changing the Scorecard for the Church* (San Francisco: Jossey-Bass, 2009), 69.

5. Harry Emerson Fosdick, *The Meaning of Prayer* (New York: Association Press, 1963), 137.

6. Ibid., 137–39.

Chapter 13: Marrying Place and People

1. Peter Kageyama, *For the Love of Cities: The Love Affair Between People and Their Places* (St. Petersburg, Fla: Creative Cities Productions, 2011), 215.

2. Sean Benesh, *View From the Urban Loft: Developing a Theological Framework for Understanding the City* (Eugene, Oreg.: Resource Publications, an imprint of Wipf and Stock, 2011), 137–38.

Chapter 14: Mutuality in Partnership

1. http://www.goodreads.com/quotes/tag/life. Accessed March 11, 2012.

2. The generation before me remembered vividly the day that JFK was assassinated in 1963. My generation remembers where they were on 9/1/01. I vividly remember July 25, 2002, the day that Rick Ferguson was tragically killed in an automobile accident on I-70 near Hays, Kansas. Some 10+ years later, his legacy is still bearing fruit in ministry.

3. Acts 29 seeks to be a movement of church-planting churches. For more information see http://www.acts29network.org/about// .

4. http://bayareachurchplanting.com/, Accessed 4/8/2012.?????

Chapter 15: Self-Aware Church Planter

1. Thomas Merton, *New Seeds of Contemplation* (New York: New Directions, 1961), 100.

2. For more on this topic or on how to assess your Ephesians 4 gifts, see http://www.theforgottenways.org/apest.

3. Dave Ferguson and Jon Ferguson, *Exponential: How You and Your Friends Can Start a Missional Church Movement* (Grand Rapids: Zondervan, 2010), 15.

4. Craig Van Gelder and Dwight J. Zscheile, *Missional Church in Perspective* (Grand Rapids: Baker Academic, 2011), 162.

5. Milfred Minatrea, *Shaped by God's Heart: The Passion and Practices of Missional Churches* (San Francisco: Jossey-Bass, 2004), 157.

6. Neil Cole, *Cultivating a Life for God* (Carol Stream, Ill.: ChurchSmart Resources, 1999), 82.

7. Ed Stetzer and Thom Rainer, *Transformational Church: Creating a New Scorecard for Congregations* (Nashville: B&H and Lifeway Research 2010), 105.

8. Alan Roxburgh and Fred Romanuk, *The Missional Leader: Equipping Your Church to Reach a Changing World* (San Francisco: Jossey-Bass, 2006), 17.

Chapter 16: Healthy Organizational Partnerships

1. John Livingston Nevius (1829–1893), *The Planting and Development of Missionary Churches* (New York: Foreign Mission Library, 1899). (Published, but not currently copyrighted. Copy on-line provided by Princeton Theological Seminary Library.)

2. Charles Allen Clark, "The National Presbyterian Church of Korea as a Test of the Validity of the Nevius Principles of Missionary Method," (Ph.D. diss., The University of Chicago, 1929), 29–30, as quoted in Wesley L. Handy, "Correlating the Nevius Method with Church Planting Movements: Early Korean Revivals as a Case Study," *Eleutheria*, vol. 2, issue 1, article 3 (2012). Available at: http://digitalcommons.liberty.edu/eleu/vol2/iss1/3.

3. The "majority world" is a current missiological term for what used to be called "third world."

4. Payne, J.D., "The Legacy of Roland Allen: Part One-His Life." Posted on May 13th, 2008. http://www.cmaresources.org/article/legacy-of-roland-allen-part1_jd-payne. Accessed 5/13/2012.

5. Ibid.

6. Ibid.

7. Kenny B. Moore, in a letter written to Veryl Henderson, SDOM State Director of Missions of CBGC, e-mailed November 6, 1996.

8. The Iban are an ancient tribe that traces their heritage to Mongolia through Genghis Khan. They were a headhunter tribe until well into the twentieth century.

While Mike and I were there, the tribe showed us their "head" collection, which was a trunk full of skulls. Most of the latest skulls came from Japanese soldiers who had invaded their island during WWII. It was a very memorable experience for both Mike and me.

Chapter 17: Loving Self Appropriately

1. This is an Allan Karr paraphrase of Luke 10:30–35.

2. The "Sermon on the Mount" is the common title given to the teaching of Jesus contained in the Gospel of Matthew, chapters 5–7. However, it is interesting that the "sermon" was not preached in a church building , but on the side of a mountain. The "congregation" was the adventurous disciples who followed Jesus up the mountain away from the larger crowd following him. The "sermon" was not even preached while standing, but was delivered while sitting down on the side of the mountain. Some traditionalists of church culture are surprised to realize this context, but it is clearly stated in Matthew 5:1–2.

3. Over thirty years later, Eagle Lake Camp is still an active and vibrant ministry. Even my children have attended. For more information, see *Eagle Lake Camps*, http://www.eaglelakecamps.com/ Accessed on March 9, 2012.

4. Lexic.us http://www.lexic.us/definition-of/Plimsoll_mark#1. Accessed March 9, 2012.

5. http://www.britannica.com/EBchecked/topic/464810/Plimsoll-line. Accessed March 9, 2012.

6. http://www.globalsecurity.org/military/library/policy/army/fm/55-17/ch7. htm. Accessed March 9, 2012.

7. John 13:3–8, *The Message.*

8. I have traveled and served churches all over the world and have been the humble receiver of much hospitality for many years. In 2012, as I taught in Burma, my Karen tribe hostess named Flora reminded me over and over again how much joy it gave her to serve me as a guest teacher. God has placed people like Flora in almost every body of Christ (church), on the globe to edify the rest of the Body. In His perfect economy, God gives some people gifts as a gift to the rest of us.

9. Commentary on passage on Students Training in Mission fundraising page, lhttp://www.blueridgestim.com/supporters2.fundraising.html. Accessed March 9, 2012.

10. Mike and Kate Morgan planted Well Springs Community Church in Aurora, Colorado. His calling is to the urban poor and necessitated raising full-time support for the model to be successful. Their integrity and character are the epitome of wholeheartedness, and I am honored and blessed to be their friend.

11. Exodus 20:8, *The Message.*

12. *The Baptist Faith and Message* (Nashville: LifeWay Press, 2000).

13. http://www.biblicalperspectives.com/books/sabbath_new_testament/5. html. Accessed March 9, 2012.

14. http://www.biblicalperspectives.com/books/sabbath_new_testament/5. html. Accessed March 9, 2012.

15. At Ethne Church Network, we have chosen to worship on Saturday evenings. We include fellowship, usually a meal, as part of our worship together with all the other usual elements of corporate worship. This often allows Sunday as a true day of rest and time with the family. In this rhythm, we are physically and spiritually recharged.

16. When I wrote this sentence, I was spending a week teaching in Burma. When I wasn't teaching, I was spending most of the rest of my time with the orphans of Taw Meh Pha orphanage in the Insein community of Rangoon, Burma. Our church has adopted them. We genuinely love those children, and they genuinely love us too.

17. The driving force behind this care were Duane and Summer Arledge, who at the time were ministering at Riverside Baptist Church, Denver. Other people were involved in this as well, like my mentor Kenny Moore. Kathy and I still reflect on the love shown to us during that time. We remember fondly how encouraged we were. If you are a sponsoring partner to a church planter, this is a very tangible way to show love and encourage.

18. This is a strong determining factor why, in our second church plant as a bi-vocational planter, we chose a more relational model of church. We knew that, with the demands of another vocation, we could not do the attractional model and still be holistically healthy.

Chapter 18: Living a Whole Way of Life

1. Dallas Willard, *The Spirit of the Disciplines: Understanding How God Changes Lives* (New York: HarperCollins, 1988), x.

2. Craig Van Gelder and Dwight Zscheile, *The Missional Church in Perspective: Mapping Trends and Shaping the Conversation* (Grand Rapids: The Missional Network, a division of Baker Academic, 2011), 147.

3. Linda Bergquist and Allan Karr, *Church Turned Inside Out: A Guide for Designers, Refiners and Re-Aligners* (San Francisco: Jossey-Bass, 2010), 64.

4. Linda remembers Brian McLaren sharing this with her many years ago.

5. Also see 1 Corinthians 1:21; 2 Corinthians 10:17; Galatians 6:14.

6. Wendell Berry, "The Body and the Earth," in *The Art of the Commonplace: The Agrarian Essays of Wendell Berry*, ed. Norman Wirzba (Washington, D.C.: Counterpoint, 2002), 133.

7. Richard Stearns, *The Hole in Our Gospel: The Answer That Changed My Life and Just Might Change the World* (Nashville: Thomas Nelson, 2009), 22.

Bibliography

Adeyemo, Tokunboh, gen. ed., *African Bible Commentary*. WordAlive Publishers: Nairobi, 2006.

Alexander, Christopher. *The Timeless Way of Building*. New York: Oxford University Press, 1979.

————. Sara Ishikawa, and Murray Silverstein. *A Pattern Language: Towns, Buildings, Construction*. New York: Oxford University Press, 1977.

All About Philosophy, "Deism-Enlightened Emptiness," http://www.allabouphilosophy.org/deism.htm, accessed 3/2/2012.

Allen, Roland. *The Ministry of the Spirit: Selected Writings*. Edited by David M. Paton. Eugene, Oreg.: Wipf and Stock, 2011.

The Baptist Faith and Message. Nashville: LifeWay Press, 2000.

Bass, Dorothy C. *Receiving the Day*. San Francisco: Jossey-Bass, 2000.

Bay Area Church Planting. http://bayareachurchplanting.com/. accessed 4/8/2012.

Benesh, Sean. *View from the Urban Loft: Developing a Theological Framework for Understanding the City*. Eugene, Oreg.: Resource Publications, 2011.

Bergquist, Linda, and Allan Karr. *Church Turned Inside Out: A Guide for Designers, Refiners, and Re-Aligners*. San Francisco: Jossey-Bass, 2010.

Berry, Wendell. *The Art of the Commonplace: Agrarian Essays of Wendell Berry*. Edited by Norman Wirzba. Washington, D.C.: Counterpoint, 2002.

Breen, Mike, and Walther P. Kallestad. *A Passionate Life*. Colorado Springs: Nexgen, 2005.

Brother Lawrence and F. Laubach. *The Practice of the Presence of God*. Sargent, Ga.: SeedSowers, 1973.

Bryant, Eric Michael. *Peppermint-filled Piñatas: Breaking Through Tolerance and Embracing Love*. Grand Rapids: Zondervan, 2007.

Chapman, Gary D. *The Five Love Languages: How to Express Heartfelt Commitment to Your Mate*. Chicago: Northfield, 1992.

Chaudhary, Nandita. *Listening to Culture: Constructing Reality from Everyday Talk*. New Delhi: Sage Publications, 2004.

Clark, Charles Allen. *The National Presbyterian Church of Korea as a Test of the Validity of the Nevius Principles of Missionary Method* (Ph.D. diss., The University of Chicago, 1929), 29–30. Quoted in Wesley L. Handy. "Correlating the Nevius Method with Church Planting Movements: Early Korean Revivals as a Case Study," *Eleutheria*: vol. 2: issue 1

(2012): article 3. Available at http://digitalcommons.liberty.edu/eleu/vol2/iss1/3.:Accessed May 8, 2012.

Clayman, Chris, and Meredith Lee. *EthNYcity: The Nations, Tongues, and Faiths of Metropolitan New York.* New York: Metro New York Baptist Association, 2010.

Cole, Neil. *Cultivating a Life for God.* Carol Stream, Ill.: ChurchSmart Resources, 1999.

Cordeiro, Wayne, Francis Chan, and Larry Osborne. *Sifted: Pursuing Growth Through Trials, Challenges, and Disappointments.* Grand Rapids: Zondervan, 2012.

Dale, Felicity. *An Army of Ordinary People: Stories of Real-Life Men and Women Simply Being the Church.* Carol Stream, Ill.: BarnaBooks, 2010.

_____. *Getting Started: A Practical Guide to Church Planting.* Clayton, Wash.: House2House Ministries, 2003.

Eagle Lake Camps. http://www.eaglelakecamps.com. Accessed on March 9, 2012.

Ethne Global Services. See http://www.ethneglobalservices.org/whoweare.html.

Ferguson, Dave, and Jon Ferguson. *Exponential: How You and Your Friends Can Start a Missional Church Movement.* Grand Rapids: Zondervan, 2010.

Florida, Richard. *The Rise of the Creative Class: And How It's Transforming Work, Leisure, Community and Everyday Life.* New York: Basic Books, 2002.

_____. *Who's Your City? How the Creative Economy Is Making Where to Live the Most Important Decision of Your Life.* New York: Basic Books, 2008.

Fosdick, Harry Emerson. *The Meaning of Being a Christian.* New York: Association Press, 1963.

Frost, Michael, and Alan Hirsch. *The Faith of Leap: Embracing a Theology of Risk, Adventure & Courage.* Grand Rapids: BakerBooks, 2011.

Gaiman, Neil. "The Kindly Ones." *The Sandman,* vol. 9. New York: Vertigo, 1996.

Global Security.Org. http://www.globalsecurity.org/military/library/policy/army/fm/55-17/ch7.htm.Accessed March 9, 2012.

Godin, Seth. *Tribes: We Need You to Lead Us.* New York: Portfolio, 2008.

Good Reads. http://www.goodreads.com/quotes/tag/life. Accessed March 11, 2012.

Gorringe, Timothy. *A Theology of the Built Environment: Justice, Empowerment, Redemption.* Cambridge: Cambridge University Press, 2002.

Hiebert, Paul G. *Anthropological Insights for Missionaries.* Grand Rapids: Baker Book House, 1985.

Hirsch, Alan, and Tim Catchim. *The Permanent Revolution: Apostolic Imagination and Practice for the 21st Century Church.* San Francisco: Jossey-Bass, 2012.

Ingram, Chip. *Good to Great in God's Eyes: 10 Practices Great Christians Have in Common.* Grand Rapids: BakerBooks, 2007.

Kageyama, Peter. *For the Love of Cities: The Love Affair Between People and Their Places.* St. Petersburg: Creative Cities Productions, 2011.

Krejcir, Richard J. *Statistics on Pastors: What Is Going on with the Pastors in America?* (Blog on site of the Francis Schaeffer Institute), http://www.intothyword.org/apps/ articles/default.asp?articleid=36562.

Lee, Jung Young. *The Trinity in Asian Perspective.* Nashville: Abingdon Press, 1996.

MacArthur, John. *Ashamed of the Gospel: When the Church Becomes Like the World.* 3rd ed. Wheaton, Ill.: Crossway Books, 2010.

Manokaran, J. N. *Christ and Missional Leaders.* Chennai, India: Mission Educational Books, 2007.

McNeal, Reggie. *Missional Renaissance: Changing the Scorecard for the Church.* San Francisco: Jossey-Bass, 2009.

Merton, Thomas. *Seeds of Contemplation.* New York: New Directions, 2007.

Minatrea, Milfred. *Shaped by God's Heart: The Passion and Practices of Missional Churches.* San Francisco: Jossey-Bass, 2004.

Moore, Kenny. E-mail from 2/20/2012.

_____. E-mail from 2/12/2012.

_____. in a letter written to Veryl Henderson, SDOM of CBGC, e-mailed November 6, 1996.

Nevius, John Livingston. *The Planting and Development of Missionary Churches.* New York: Foreign Mission Library, 1899 (Published, but not currently copyrighted. Copy on-line provided by Princeton Theological Seminary Library).

Peterson, Eugene H. *Working the Angles: The Shape of Pastoral Integrity.* Grand Rapids: W.B. Eerdmans, 1987.

Plimsoll Line. http://www.britannica.com/EBchecked/topic/464810/Plimsoll-line. Accessed March 9, 2012.

Plimsoll Mark. http://www.lexic.us/definition-of/Plimsoll_mark#1. Accessed March 9, 2012.

Roxburgh, Alan, and Fred Romanuk. *The Missional Leader: Equipping Your Church to Reach a Changing World.* San Francisco: Jossey-Bass, 2006.

Saint Patrick, from *The Confession of Saint Patrick: Book of Armagh, 450 A.D.* Academy for Ancient Texts. Ancient texts library. http://www.ancienttexts.org/library/celtic/ctexts/p01.html. Accessed May 20, 2012.

Sire, James W. *The Universe Next Door: A Guide Book to World Views.* 3d ed. Downers Grove, Ill.: InterVarsity Press, 1997.

_____. *Naming the Elephant: Worldview as a Concept.* Downers Grove, Ill.: InterVarsity Press, 2004.

Smith, Steve and Kai, Ying. *T4T: A Discipleship Re-Revolution.* Monument, Colo.: WIGTake, 2011.

Solnit, Rebecca. *Infinite City: A San Francisco Atlas.* Berkeley: University of California Press, 2010.

Stearns, Richard. *The Hole in Our Gospel: The Answer That Changed My Life and Might Just Change the World.* Nashville: Thomas Nelson, 2009.

Stetzer, Ed, and Thom Rainer. *Transformational Church: Creating a New Scorecard for Congregations.* Nashville: B&H and Lifeway Research, 2010.

Student Training in Missions. "Perspectives on Fundraising," http://www.blueridgestim.com/supporters2.fundraising.html. Accessed March 9, 2012.

Tozer, A.W. "For Pastors Only," *Alliance Weekly* (May 6, 1950).

Van Gelder, Craig, and Dwight J. Zscheile. *The Missional Church in Perspective: Mapping Trends and Shaping the Conversation.* Grand Rapids: The Missional Network, a Division of Baker Academic, 2011.

Virgil. *The Georgics.* Translation by Smith Palmer Bovie. Chicago: The University of Chicago Press, 1966.

Warren, Rick. *Radicalis Conference, Saddleback Church.* Lake Forrest, Calif., Feb. 22–25, 2011.

Willard, Dallas. *The Spirit of the Disciplines: Understanding How God Changes Lives.* San Francisco: Harper & Row, 1988.

Wolfe, Thomas. "The Far and the Near" was published first in *Cosmopolitan* magazine in 1935 and later reprinted in Thomas Wolfe's book of collected stories, *From Death to Morning.* New York: C. Scribner's Sons, 1935.

Index